Santa's Loading Dock QUILT

MARY BUVIA

American Quilter's Society
P. O. Box 3290 • Paducah, KY 42002-3290
www.AmericanQuilter.com

Located in Paducah, Kentucky, the American Quilter's Society (AQS) is dedicated to promoting the accomplishments of today's quilters. Through its publications and events, AQS strives to honor today's quiltmakers and their work and to inspire future creativity and innovation in quiltmaking.

EXECUTIVE BOOK EDITOR: ANDI MILAM REYNOLDS
COPY EDITOR: CHRYSTAL ABHALTER
GRAPHIC DESIGN: ELAINE WILSON
ILLUSTRATIONS: LYNDA SMITH
COVER DESIGN: MICHAEL BUCKINGHAM
QUILT PHOTOGRAPHY: CHARLES R. LYNCH

Additional copies of this book may be ordered from the American Quilter's Society, PO Box 3290, Paducah, KY 42002-3290, or online at www.AmericanQuilter.com.

Text © 2012, Author, Mary Buvia
Artwork © 2012, American Quilter's Society

Library of Congress Cataloging-in-Publication Data

Buvia, Mary.
  Santa's loading dock quilt / by Mary Buvia.
    pages cm
  Summary: "Recreate this masterpiece quilt to celebrate the holiday season! Includes 90 patterns, many at full size. Even beginning quilters can make this quilt with Mary's clear instructions and the numerous detailed photographs. Patterns can be used separately to decorate stockings, tote bags, sweaters-the possibilities are endless!"--Provided by publisher.
  ISBN 978-1-60460-033-9
  1. Quilting--Patterns. 2. Patchwork--Patterns. 3. Christmas decorations. I. Title.
  TT835.B896 2012
  746.46--dc23
                    2012023766

Contents

LEFT: **THE LOADING DOCK**
87" x 86", made by the author

Introduction

My wish is that you enjoy these whimsical and fun patterns as much as I have enjoyed creating THE LOADING DOCK quilt and this book. My sincere desire is to bring a smile to your face and happiness to your heart while you create your own vision of Christmas.

This book is a truly unique and original collection of designs depicting the holiday spirit as may be envisioned through a child's mind-eye, no matter his or her age. Please feel free to rearrange the objects and change colors to best suit yourself. Have a great time bringing these little characters to life!

Feel free to use one or more elements to decorate something smaller than a full-size quilt. Appliqué an elf on a "Welcome" sign for your front door, or sew a horn on the stocking of an aspiring musician! So many elements—so many ways to use them!

Many facets of this quilt were discussed with my late husband, a wonderful and creative artist who helped guide my hands and heart during the quiltmaking process. THE LOADING DOCK was a large part of our lives during his last year of illness. Stitched into this quilt are the hearts and souls of two people—Bob and me.

The overwhelming response by people who have viewed the quilt has been instrumental in getting me through the tough year following his passing. For this encouragement I can only say, "Thank You!"

I truly consider THE LOADING DOCK to be my masterpiece—my complete heart and soul. It was honored with Master Quilt status in 2011 by the National Quilting Association. For that award I am most grateful.

To everyone who may wish to recreate even a small portion of this detailed piece, thanks to the vision of the American Quilter's Society for publishing this book, I wish you every success and, most of all, much enjoyment.

"THE LOADING DOCK"©
87" x 86"
Mary Susan Buvia
Address
City, State
Phone Number

Began: 12-25-2009
Finished: 12-25-2010

DEDICATED TO
my late husband

Robert D. Buvia
8-11-1929 to 11-5-2010

Largely hand-made during the many long hours sitting with him receiving chemo treatments. Finished quilting, through many tears, after losing Bob to a long battle with cancer. The design was created on Christmas day, 2009 in tribute to his favorite holiday.

Love Forever - Mary

General Directions

This chapter is all you need to make THE LOADING DOCK or to use its appliqué elements as you like. Please read it through before sewing for best results. If a given pattern requires special instructions, those are included with that appliqué element.

Overview

I use freezer paper, appliqué glue, short pins, and a master pattern traced from the full-size original pattern (Fig. 1). Unwaxed butcher paper is used for all drawings.

The advantage of retracing each appliqué pattern is to work from a small pattern rather than from the bulk or the full-size paper pattern, which then remains intact as a placement guide for the completed appliqué elements. Appliqués prepared this way may be sewn to the background by hand or machine.

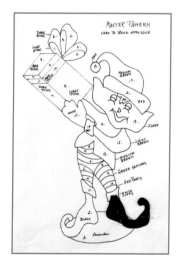 

FIG. 1. Master pattern (left) traced from the full-size original pattern (right)

Fabrics

I recommend prewashing fabrics, as many reds, greens, and black and white colors are used for these patterns. Prewashing removes excess dye so that darker colors will not bleed onto lighter colors during a later washing.

Remove the fabrics from the dryer, spray starch onto the back side of the fabrics, and iron them smooth. Starching will add body to the fabrics without the use of chemicals, aiding in more accurate cutting, piecing, and quilting without the edges raveling.

Use quality fabrics to minimize the shadowing of tiny, turned-under seams. My choice of fabric for THE LOADING DOCK was the Fairy Frost line by Michael Miller Fabrics (Fig. 2). This line is made of a high quality fabric that offers a large number of colors and value ranges, and is still available as this book goes to press in Summer of 2012. The "pearlized crinkle sheer iridescent" fabrics called for in the snowflake and icicle designs are available in the special occasion section at most fabric stores.

Technique Information

Certain patterns must be enlarged to achieve the size of the original quilt; this is indicated on each design. All of the patterns may be enlarged or reduced to meet your design needs.

For some patterns, marking stitching lines on the fabrics will be helpful. Examples include the smile and nose lines on elf faces and mouth lines on teddy bears. Stitch these areas before quilting. Select your favorite fabric marking tool, or try my preference, Clover® Water Soluble Marker.

FIG. 2. Fairy Frost line by Michael Miller Fabrics

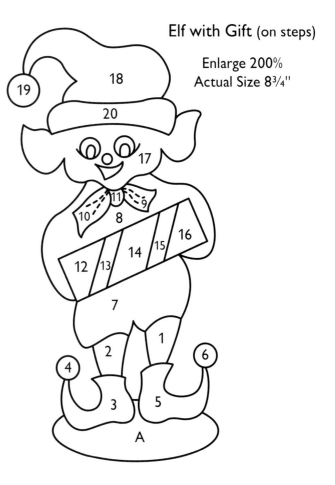

Elf with Gift (on steps)

Enlarge 200%
Actual Size 8¾"

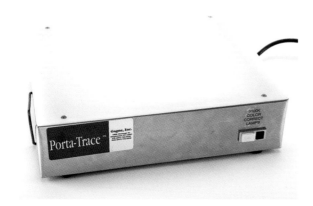

FIG. 3. Light box

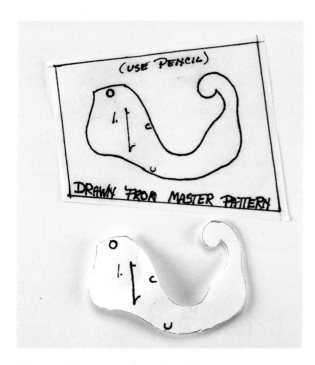

FIG. 4. Create templates from the master pattern.

Free-motion stitching outlines eyes, noses, and mouth areas on many patterns. To set the sewing machine, drop the feed dogs, select a quilting or embroidery foot, set the straight stitch at 0, and put the presser foot in the down position while stitching.

Use a small machine embroidery hoop to aid in controlling the stitching. **Tear-away stabilizer must always be used on the wrong side of the fabric.** This outline technique is simply free-motion quilting without batting.

A light box will help you view the master pattern placement of the appliqué pieces when using dark fabrics. Lightly tape the master pattern to the light box and pin the pieces into position (Fig. 3).

Appliqué Preparation

Freezer-paper turned edges work well to achieve a beautiful, smooth, turned-edge finish. A raw-edge appliqué technique that showcases your satin-stitch skills may also be used.

Using either technique, the appliqué pieces are glued into place following numerical order on master pattern. Remove from paper pattern and stitch glued areas. When completed, glue appliqué onto background fabric and stitch perimeter. Remove excess fabric on reverse side creating a flat, single layer for the quilt top.

Note that you will reverse the patterns for either method, since the freezer paper will be ironed onto the back of the fabric.

FREEZER-PAPER TURNED EDGES

To prepare freezer paper for turned-edge appliqué patterns, cut two pieces approximately 20" x 20". Using a hot dry setting, iron both pieces separately, wax side down, to preshrink the paper. Then iron both pieces together, wax sides down, to create a heavy form for the fabric pieces (Fig. 4). This two-step technique eliminates bubbles in the template and will aid in achieving perfectly turned appliqué edges.

RAW-EDGE

For raw-edge appliqué, cut patterns to exact size, then select a zigzag satin stitch or decorative stitch to finish the raw edges. Place tearaway stabilizer behind the fabric at all times. Sew a sample to select the stitch, width, and length to achieve the desired coverage of edges. Reduce the top tension so the bobbin thread is not visible on the top of the appliqué (Fig. 5).

Master Pattern Directions

Carefully trace the entire appliqué unit from the full-size butcher paper pattern using a fine point black marker. This smaller size will become your master pattern.

Do not separate the pattern pieces. Note any thoughts and directions in the margins of this master pattern, such as a key for values (L = light, etc.).

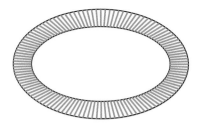

FIG. 5. SATIN STITCH Edge: Cut exact shape, glue along outside edge, place in position and stitch. Below, bell with some satin stitch edges.

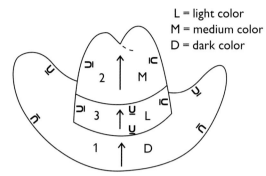

L = light color
M = medium color
D = dark color

FIG. 6

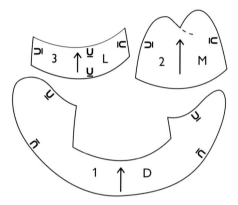

FIG. 7

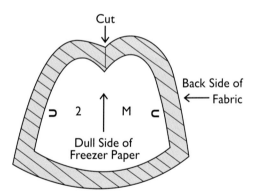

Cut

Back Side of Fabric

Dull Side of Freezer Paper

FIG. 8

Note that you will reverse the patterns for either method, since the freezer paper will be ironed onto the back of the fabric.

To use the master pattern:

1 Mark the straight grain lines on each pattern piece using a ruler. By following the grain line of the fabric while cutting, the finished piece will hang properly (Fig. 6).

2 Mark all edges to be turned under with an underlined "U" (so you don't mistake it for a "C") and all edges to be left open with an "O" (do not turn these under). In most areas, this will indicate places to be covered by something else.

3 Pattern piece numbers indicate the lay-out order of fabric pieces (Fig. 6). The indicators and grain and under directions will aid in understanding each pattern piece when working with several patterns at one time.

4 Using paper and pencil, redraw each pattern piece separately using butcher paper, leaving ½" around each piece for ease in pinning and cutting smaller pattern pieces (Fig. 7).

5 Cut pattern pieces apart, leaving a ⅜" margin for freezer-paper appliqué, or cutting right on the line for raw-edge appliqué.

6 Place the paper pattern onto the prepared freezer paper, shiny side UP. Pin carefully, using short straight pins that will not protrude into your cutting area. Cut on the drawn pencil line through paper and freezer paper. *The shape that you cut at this point will be the exact shape of your fabric appliqué piece.* Take care to cut with accuracy.

7 Again, transfer all your written grain and other directions to the DULL side of the freezer paper pattern, noting that these directions will be in reverse of the paper notations.

8 Iron the SHINY side (waxed) of the freezer paper to the BACK (reverse) side of the fabric until it adheres, being careful not to overheat the paper and fabric to prevent damage.

9 Cut the fabric around the freezer paper template, allowing a ¼" seam allowance (Fig. 8) for smaller appliqués and approximately ⅜" allowance for larger appliqués such as the sleigh, continents, floor, and globe, to name a few.

10 Using a mini iron (Fig. 9) and spray starch (or diluted *Sew Stable*), wet the seam area marked "U" using a small, stiff paint brush. Avoid getting the solution on the freezer paper template; no need to saturate this area. Iron down the seam just to the freezer paper line. Gently roll the fabric to the template line, as forcing may cause the template to curl, resulting in inaccurate shapes.

Keeping the iron down on the fabric and working in a small seam area, glide the iron over the turned edge. Raising and lowering the iron will only dry the area quickly, and will not secure the seam to the template.

When all marked edges have been ironed, remove the freezer paper. While this process may appear to be a bit overwhelming, it will become easy after practice and will expand your creative options.

Tip:
Spray a small amount of starch into the cap of the can to easily dip a ¼" stiff, flat-ended paint brush into the solution.

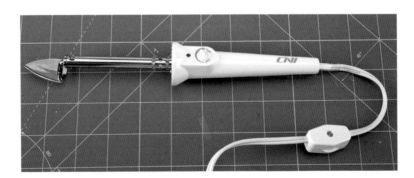

FIG. 9

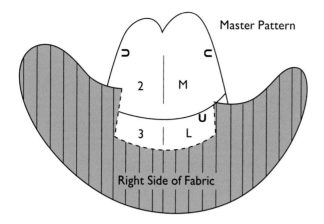

FIG. 10

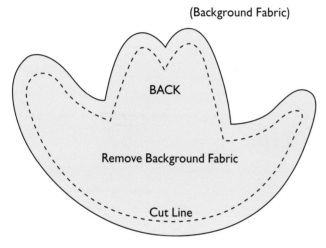

FIG. 11

PLACEMENT ON MASTER PATTERN

My technique allows for a beautiful single layer appliqué with no bulk on the quilt face.

Work the pieces from the back to the front of the design in numerical order. Place a fabric pattern piece on the master pattern, noting that the turned edge fits the pattern (Fig. 10). Following the numbered order, pin appliqué pieces onto the paper with small straight pins.

Build the entire design up to the front pieces. Lift each turned seam line carefully to place a thin bead of appliqué glue. Press and hold down until the glue adheres to the fabric. Using this technique, carefully glue and construct the entire appliqué.

When the glue is set, lift the design from the paper master pattern. This appliqué is now ready to be stitched by hand. Some areas may be machine pieced, if desired.

Trim each seam of the completely stitched appliqué on the underside to approximately ⅛" to remove excess fabric. Larger appliqué pieces may be trimmed to ¼" seam allowances.

At this point, the completed appliqué can be pinned onto the background fabric in the desired position. Place a narrow bead of appliqué glue around the entire perimeter and allow to dry. If desired, a warm iron can be used to set the glue quickly. Hand or machine stitch the appliqué onto the background fabric. Carefully trim out the excess background fabric to within ⅛" (for very small seams) to ¼" (for larger seam allowances) (Fig. 11).

Special Instructions for Completed Toy Appliqués

Place completed toy appliqués onto toy bag liner background fabric (see Toy Placement Order on page 85). Pin toys into place, noting the areas that are under or over other toys.

Glue each edge of toy into place. Hand or machine stitch each toy using matching thread colors; trim away excess fabric on reverse side to within ⅛" of seam line.

After all toys are hand stitched into position, place tear-away stabilizer behind all areas to be satin stitched, one at a time. When stitching is completed, pull thread tails to the reverse side, tie, and clip to within ½". Remove stabilizer and trim away all excess fabric on reverse side to within ⅛" of seam lines.

All toys should be stitched in the ditch during the quilting process. Use a neutral color thread to tightly stitch the areas of the inner bag liner that are visible when all toys are in place.

Threads and Needles

Use matching 100-wt. silk threads for both hand and machine appliqué. These fine threads bury themselves into the fabric and simply disappear. I recommend Superior Kimono Silk™ 100-wt. thread; a range of 80 colors is available (Fig. 12). Short tiny stitches are secure for either hand or machine sewing and add no bulk in the seam allowances.

FIG. 12

For hand appliqué, use an appliqué needle. This needle is generally short, thin, and very sharp. For machine piecing, appliqué, or quilting with silk thread, a size 70/10 or 80/12 topstitch or metallic needle works well to carry the threads without breakage.

Pull thread tails to the back of each completed appliqué. For ease in pulling thread tails to the reverse side of the fabric, use a self-threading or easy-thread needle (Fig. 13). These needles have an extra slotted opening at the top end. Carefully snap the thread tails into this eye and glide the needle (with threads attached) to the reverse side of the fabric.

Pull all thread tails to the back side, tie, and clip to within ¼"–½". Remove stabilizer.

FIG. 13

Quilt Assembly

THE LOADING DOCK measures 87" x 86". I followed the full-size pattern in most every section of this quilt; however, I slightly rearranged a few elves for a more pleasing balance.

I suggest you follow this quilt assembly order, then rearrange the appliqués to suit your personal vision:

1 Blue globe upper background

2 Continents

3 Snowflakes

4 Window (completed)

5 Outside decorative window trim

6 Purple floor and connecting horizontal sashing

7 Shop area:

    a. brick walls

    b. door (completed)

    c. wall lamp

    d. sign

    e. left wall behind sled and stocking

    f. sled

    g. stocking

    h. landing and steps

    i. gold grill work (on blue background)

    j. shop sign bell

    k. left narrow purple frame between wall and stones

    l. stone wall

    m. outside left purple narrow frame

Add shop area to blue upper background/floor

8 Name tag left section (grill work, name tags, bells and bows)

9 Narrow green connector (white trim is narrow couched decorative cording)

Add name tag section to upper blue background/floor

10 Clock and connector chain

11 Sleigh (including bell, horn, toys in bag, and bow)

    Toy Placement Order:

    a. tennis racquet

    b. skis

    c. football

    d. Christmas tree

    e. horn

    f. teddy bear (under horn)

    g. sailboat

    h. guitar

    i. crayon box

    j. round ball

    k. doll

    l. cradle

    m. teddy bear (lower right)

    n. package (lower right)

    o. spinning top

    p. nutcracker

    q. blocks

    r. dog

    s. package (upper left)

    t. Raggedy Ann

    u. drum sticks

    v. drum

    w. train

    x. panda bear

12 Elves, floor packages, ice skates, and teddy bear on steps

13 Holly and berries draped across top of completed quilt face

8 Name tag section

6 Floor

9 Green connector

10 Clock & chain

2 Continents

5 Trim

4 Window

13 Holly & berries

3 Snowflakes

1 Globe

7 Shop area

12 Elves, packages, skates

11 Sleigh

Quilting Decisions

As I studied the finished quilt top, I knew that the quilting must enhance and "pop" each and every area to complete the feel of this design.

Normally, I draw quilting ideas on the full-size pattern, then make sample quilting to check for results. In this case, however, decisions were made after careful consideration of each area at a time. For example, snowflake quilting designs were added to complement the appliquéd snowflakes (Fig. 14). Small curved quilting was added to the blue background to suggest moving water. Santa's seat was quilted in the ditch between appliquéd sections to create a tufted appearance.

Santa himself had to appear somewhere in this quilt; however, I did not want him to be obvious. In the "wood" piece at the back of his chair, you will find Santa rising from a snow-capped chimney in quilted form (Fig. 15). See page 92 for this quilting design.

FIG. 14. Snowflake quilting designs

FIG. 15. Santa himself!

The lavender floor was quilted using a simple design to create a wood grain illusion (Fig. 16). The toy bag was intended to appear as burlap fabric; therefore, quilting lines were added following the shape of the bag. More detailed quilting style was created for the sleigh, as it was to be not only fancy, but also the focal point of this quilt (See page 75).

Outline quilting was sufficient around many of the small appliqué sections so as not to flatten the objects. The door and wall to the toy shop area required a more textured appearance, but I kept within the same type and density of quilting (Fig. 17).

In short, consider the overall goal of your quilt, but give each individual area's quilting unique consideration. Think about loft, texture, detail, and whether you want the quilting to appear obvious or subtle.

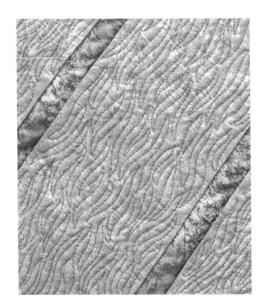

ABOVE: **FIG. 16.** Wood grain in floor

RIGHT: **FIG. 17.** Door and wall to toy shop

Patterns

BACKGROUND

Order of Assembly

- **21** Globe
- **22** Floor
- **24** Continents
- **29** "North"
- **30** Snowflakes
- **34** Red/gold ironwork
- **38** Clock/chain
- **41** Reindeer names, tags, jingle bells, and bows
- **44** Holly vine

The finished quilt size is 87" x 86". It is constructed in three background sections: floor, globe, and toy shop area. The column of reindeer names is attached as if it were a border.

Use the freezer paper technique described in General Directions for each section to eliminate stretching of the bias edges.

Globe

Create a large pieced circle 53" in diameter (finished) for the globe. To make a template the correct size, begin by drawing a horizontal line and a vertical line in the center of the master quilt pattern. From the vertical line, begin on the left side. Measuring approximately 5" away from the vertical line, draw a soft curved line as you would see on a globe. Continue this line out to the edge of the background. Fold the pattern down the vertical line and trace the curved line to the right side.

Use the same process to draw curved lines at the top and bottom of the horizontal straight line. Following General Directions, make a freezer paper template for each piece.

Place lighter blue values in the center, working out in all directions to the darker blue values. Some of these transitions may be covered by appliqués.

Each section is glued together. The globe pieces may be machine pieced. Trim each seam allowance when stitching is completed to within ¼" of seam line before adding another section.

When all sections are completed, center and pin to master pattern. Stitch to lavender floor lower background with a connecting 1¾" sashing that may be a blue/lavender color.

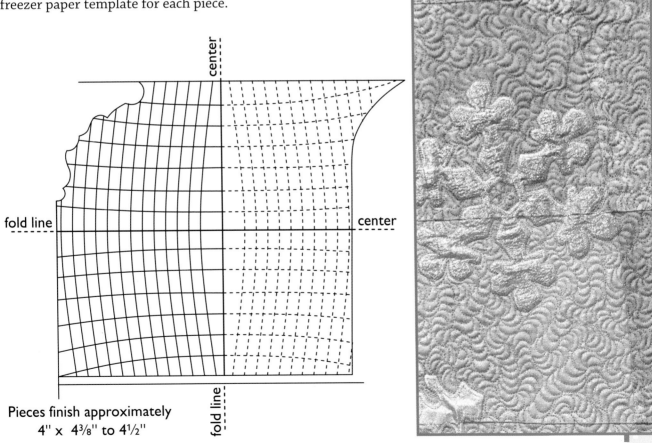

center

fold line

center

fold line

Pieces finish approximately
4" x 4⅜" to 4½"

Floor

The floor area was drawn in perspective leading back to the toy shop. I used several values of purples to create depth and shadows.

The darkest value is at the back near steps and left blue background areas. Medium to dark values are under the sleigh for depth. The lightest values are in the center front at the widest point of the boards in order to appear most forward.

All of the board and sashing sections were cut on the straight grain of the fabric so the completed quilt would hang properly.

Set the floor section aside until you can join it to the globe section.

Size of floor area is shown unquilted.

Begin construction by stitching all sections of boards together. Starting at lower right, add 1" (finished size) sashing and continue to upper left.

Freezer paper template technique is suggested for the narrow sashings, turning under both long sides. Place boards on full-size pattern and glue sashings into place for stitching. This process eliminates stretching of fabric pieces during stitching.

Color and Yardage

1. Light purple . . . . 2 yards
2. Medium light purple . . 1½ yards
3. Medium purple . . . . . . 2½ yards
4. Dark purple . . . . 1½ yards
5. Blue Purple . . . . 1½ yards

Note:

Extra yardage is allowed for cutting bias pieces.

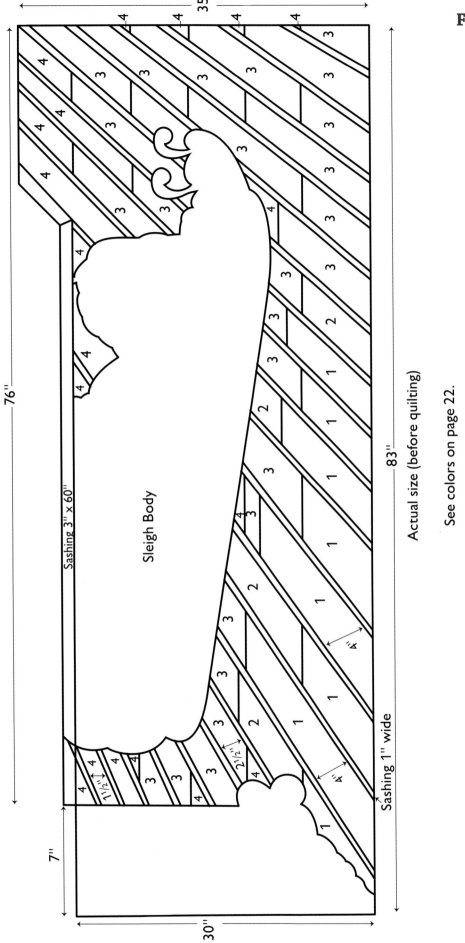

35"

4   4   4   4

76"

Sashing 3" x 60"

Sleigh Body

83"

Actual size (before quilting)

See colors on page 22.

Sashing 1" wide

7"

1½"

2½"

1½"

4"

4"

30"

Continents

Appliqué Piece	Color	Piece Size
All Continents	Light or medium tan	
Center right group		11" x 21"
Lower right continent		12" x 16"
Lower left continent		14" x 22"
Upper left continent		14" x 22"
Upper right continent		14" x 28"

Follow General Directions to assemble continents.

Place, glue, and stitch appliqués onto background. Note that upper continents will extend into binding area. Right and left lower continents will be placed under other appliqué pieces.

Remove excess background fabric to within ¼" of seam line.

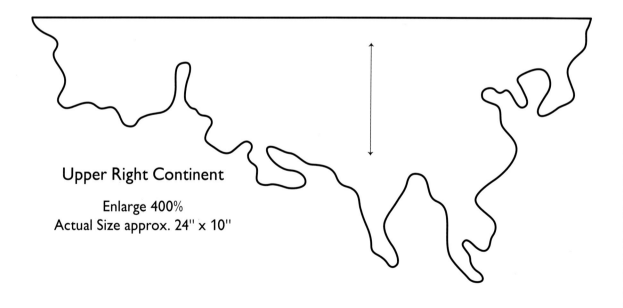

Upper Right Continent

Enlarge 400%
Actual Size approx. 24" x 10"

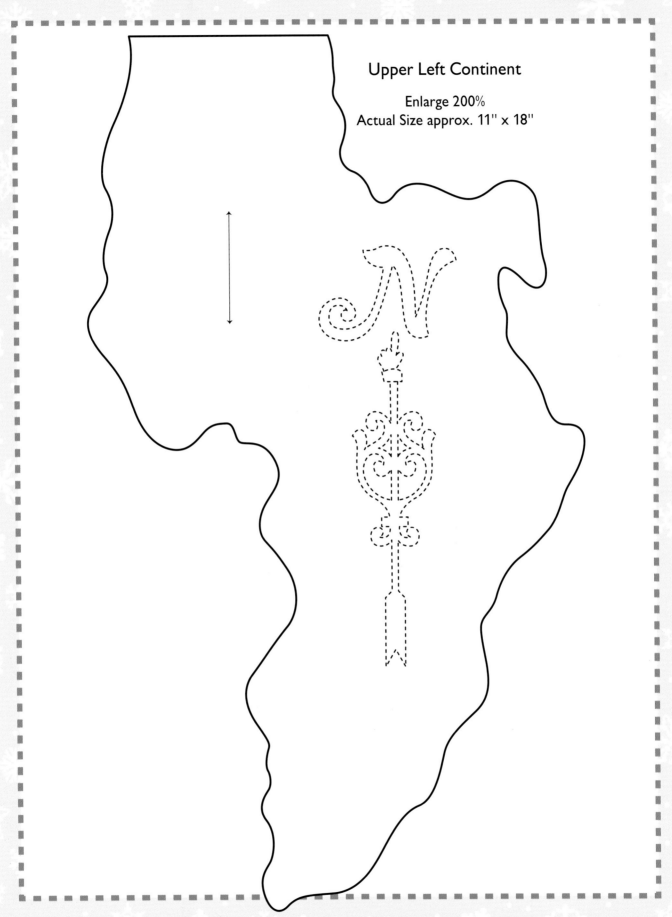

Upper Left Continent

Enlarge 200%
Actual Size approx. 11" x 18"

Continents

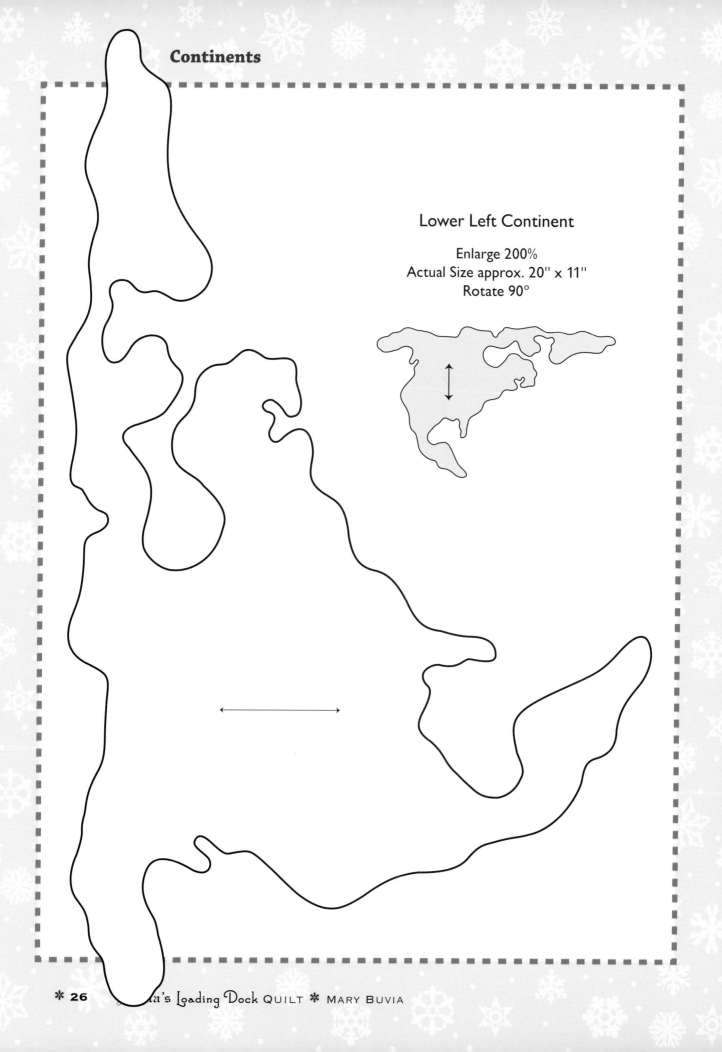

Lower Left Continent

Enlarge 200%
Actual Size approx. 20" x 11"
Rotate 90°

Center Right Group

Enlarge 200%
Actual Size approx. 8" x 14"

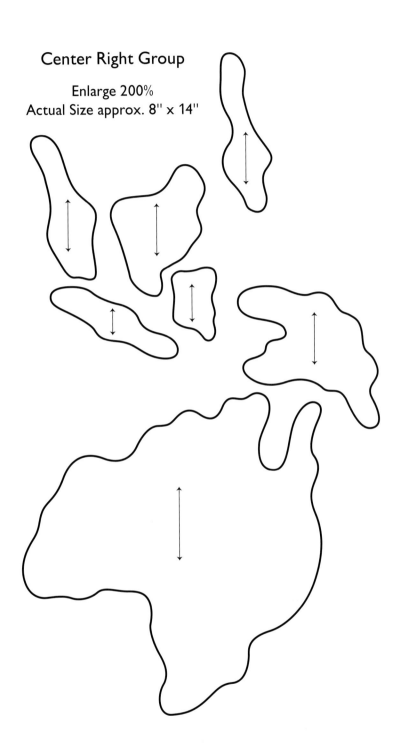

Continents

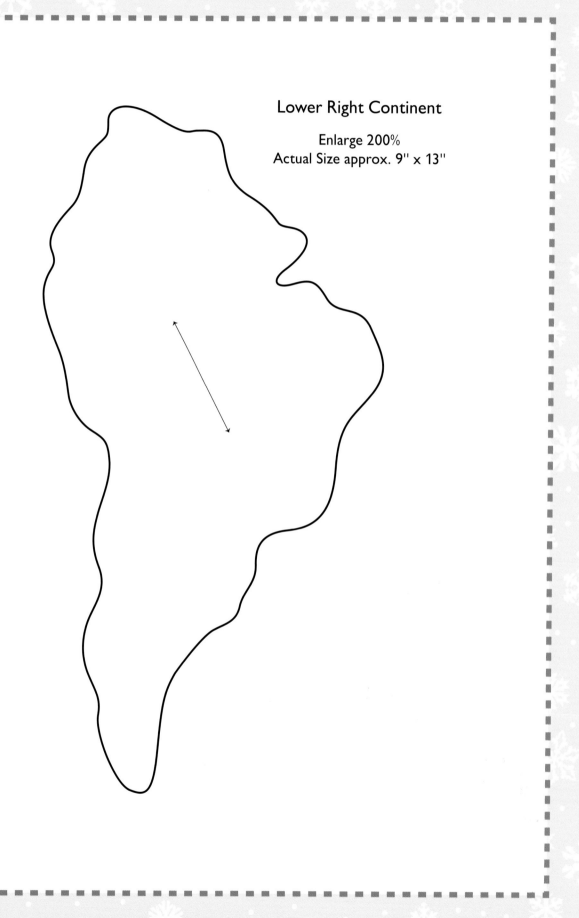

Lower Right Continent

Enlarge 200%
Actual Size approx. 9" x 13"

"North"

Appliqué Piece	Color	Piece Size
1	Red	4" x 5"
2	Light green	2" x 2"
3	Dark green	2" x 2"
4	Black	5" x 9"

Cut all appliqué pieces exact pattern size. Place paper pattern under background fabric. Use a light box, if necessary, in order to see placement of pieces. Position and glue all sections. Allow glue to dry or press with warm iron. Place tear-away stabilizer behind entire appliqué.

Satin stitch all sections. You may wish to narrow the width of the satin stitch in very narrow areas. There will be starting and stopping in the black section.

It is not necessary to remove any background fabric under appliqué.

North Symbol

Shown at 100%

Snowflakes

Appliqué Piece	Color	Piece Size
	Pearlized crinkle sheer iridescent film (or fabric of your choice) in white, light pink, light yellow, light blue, light green, light purple	
Snowflake diameter		
4"		6" x 6"
4½"		7" x 7"
5"		7" x 7"
5½"		8" x 8"
6½"		9" x 9"

Follow General Directions to create snowflakes.

Enlarge or shrink the 12 snowflake designs to suit your vision of your quilt. I placed 24 snowflakes on THE LOADING DOCK.

Press light fusible web to one side of sheer fabric using medium iron setting. Use short straight pins to hold cut-out paper snowflake template onto paper side of web. Lightly trace entire design onto fusible web paper. Cut on drawn line. Remove paper and apply sealant such as Dritz® Fray Check to edges to prevent raveling.

Position the snowflake on the quilt top. Using a pressing cloth on top of the appliqué, press with a medium warm iron. *Do not touch iron directly to the film fabric, as this may cause fabric damage.* If there are areas of the snowflake that do not adhere to the fabric, carefully lift these

sections and apply a small amount of appliqué glue. Allow to dry.

A tight satin stitch setting will cut delicate film fabric, so use a more open setting. Satin stitch snowflake into place. *Do not remove any background fabric.* Remove stabilizer and iron appliqué using a pressing cloth on film fabric.

When quilt top is ready for quilting, stitch around entire snowflake close to the appliqué without touching satin stitching. Dense background stitching creates a more visual snowflake appliqué.

Snowflakes
Shown at 50%

Actual snowflakes range in diameter from 4"–6½". Enlarge or shrink patterns to suit your quilt design.

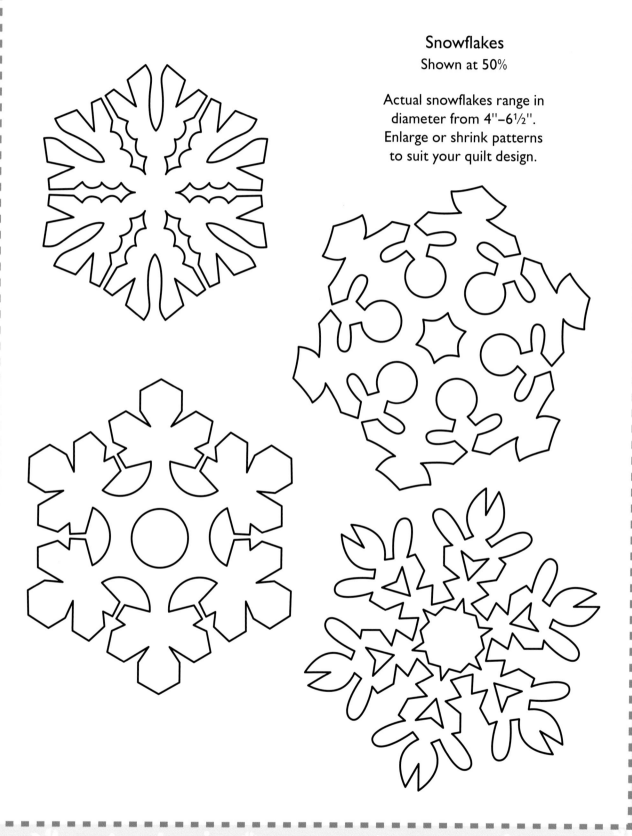

Snowflakes

Shown at 50%

Actual snowflakes range in diameter from 4"–6½". Enlarge or shrink patterns to suit your quilt design.

Snowflakes
Shown at 50%

Actual snowflakes range in
diameter from 4"–6½".
Enlarge or shrink patterns
to suit your quilt design.

Red/gold Ironwork

APPLIQUÉ PIECE	COLOR	PIECE SIZE
Inside border	Green	30" x 90"*
Background	Red	30" x 90"
Ironwork	Gold	30" x 90"
Outer border	Blue	3" x 90" **

* Cut as one piece on straight of grain to help quilt hang straight

** Finished size 1¼" x 87½"

Follow General Directions to trace one-piece templates of all appliqué pieces. Dotted lines near top of ironwork pattern indicate placement for clock chain.

Cut red section adding ¼" seam allowances to both sides; add ½" seam allowances to top and bottom.

Satin stitch inside border into place; cut both sides the actual size of the pattern adding ½" to both top and bottom. If desired, white piping or cording may be placed and stitched between the red and green pieces.

Cut outer border adding ¼" to inside edge and ½" to left edge, top, and bottom. Piece outer border to red background using ¼" seam allowances. Press seam towards outer border.

Make 1 pattern from both ironwork patterns. Place pattern onto gold fabric and carefully cut the exact shape. Glue or fuse ironwork in place. Satin stitch.

Place, glue, and stitch all completed name tags, bows, and jingle bells. See pages 35–37 for patterns.

Sew completed appliqué to floor/globe background. Satin stitch.

Red/gold Ironwork

Enlarge 400%
Actual Size 20" x 87½"

Green narrow border
Red background
Gold ironwork

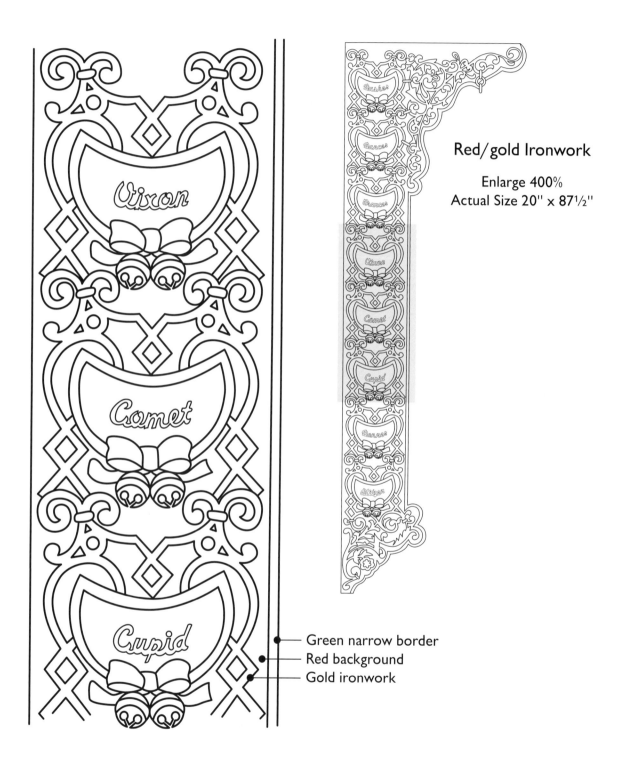

Red/gold Ironwork

Enlarge 400%
Actual Size 20" x 87½"

- Green narrow border
- Red background
- Gold ironwork

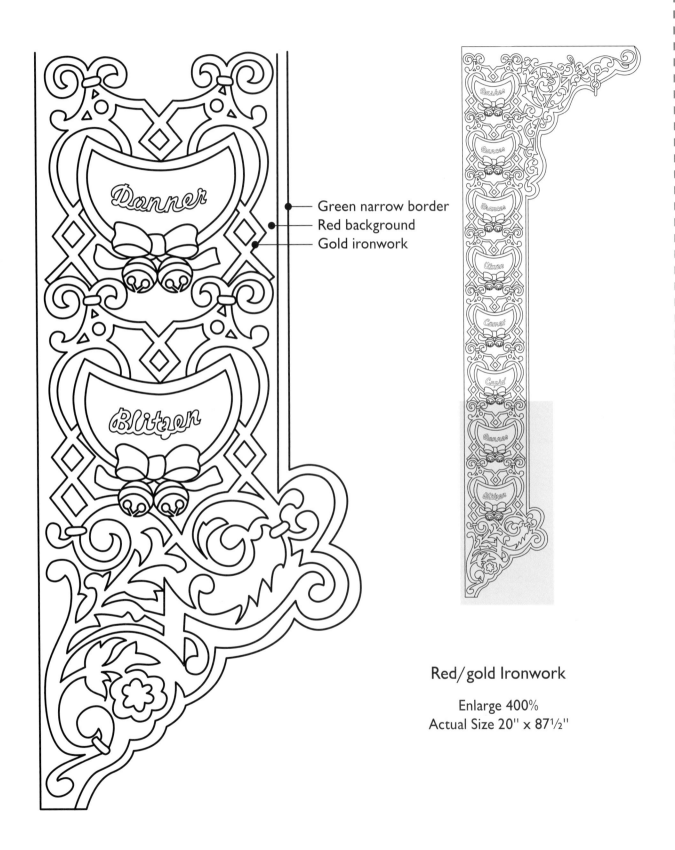

Green narrow border
Red background
Gold ironwork

Red/gold Ironwork

Enlarge 400%
Actual Size 20" x 87½"

Clock / Chain

Appliqué Piece	Color	Piece Size
Numbers and letters	Red	12" x 12"
A	Red	¼ yard
B	White	18" x 18"
C	Bright yellow	12" x 12"
Clock hands	Black	6" x 6"
1, 2	Light green	20" x 20"
3, 4, 9, 10, 12, 18	Dark green	12" x 18"
5, 6, 7, 8, 11, 13, 14, 15, 16, 17	Red	18" x 22"
19 (ornamental top and chain)	Medium gold	15" x 18"
Background face of clock	Soft gold	20" x 20"

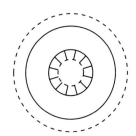

FIG. 2.

FIG. 1.

Follow General Directions to assemble clock in three sections—small candy ring center, large candy ring, and clock face and numbers with these exceptions:

Cut small center white ring (piece B) adding ¼" seam allowance to both outside edges (Fig. 1).

Cut red (piece A) candy cane pieces adding seam allowances to both outside edges (Fig. 2); glue in place onto white ring following master pattern.

Satin stitch red candy cane pieces on both long sides only.

Glue candy cane circle onto gold center. Stitch circle by hand or machine. Set aside.

Make the large candy ring the same way; set aside.

There are two ways to construct the clock face and numbers:

Prepare light green piece 1 (under numbered circles). Cut a solid light green circle; mark the division lines with a water-soluble marker. Couch over a narrow cord to accent lines, or use decorative stitching.

OR

Glue together fabric sections and machine piece all wedges.

Once the clock face is complete, add small circles for clock numbers. Trim excess fabric from back of circles. Continue constructing clock by adding numbers (see pattern), gluing the face onto the large candy ring, then onto the clock face background.

Add red borders, left side green shadow, clock hands, and center circle (piece A).

Cut holly leaves and berries to exact pattern size. Satin stitch all edges.

Cut upper decorative clock piece (piece 19) to exact pattern size. Glue onto clock face ONLY where the piece touches colors red and soft gold. Satin stitch when the finished clock is placed onto the background fabric.

Follow General Directions to assemble the lower clock, except cut piece 11 (red) to exact shape. Glue to green shadow (piece 10). Pieces 11 and 13 (red) will be satin stitched to finish edges. Machine or hand stitch piece 10 to border 7 where they touch.

Continue assembling lower clock. Cut and place "Dec 24" (see pattern). Using tear-away stabilizer behind green fabric, satin stitch the letters and numbers. Remove stabilizer.

Sew entire lower section to clock face at border piece 16.

Place finished clock onto background fabric; glue outside edges in place. Satin stitch the ornamental decoration (top). Stitch balance of outside clock by hand. On wrong side of fabric, trim away all excess fabrics in all areas.

Glue on chain to desired length. Glue upper ornament where it touches background fabric. Satin stitch entire ornament and chain.

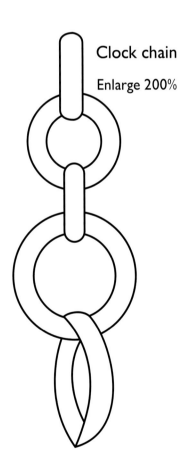

Clock chain

Enlarge 200%

Clock / Chain

Clock

Enlarge 200%
Actual Size 17½"
(not including chain)

Reindeer Names, Tags, Jingle Bells, and Bows

Appliqué Piece	Color	Piece Size
Reindeer Names	Red	24" x 60"
Name Tags (8)		
1	Light green (7" x 9" each)	60" x 75"
2	Medium blue (5" x 8" each)	40" x 65"
Jingle Bells (16)		
1	Medium gray or silver	24" x 40"
2	Dark gray	16" x 32"
3	Black	16" x 32"
Bows (8)		
1, 2	Light yellow	16" x 32"
3, 4, 5	Medium yellow	16" x 48"
6, 7	Dark yellow	16" x 32"

Prepare reindeer name appliqués using raw-edge appliqué. Set aside.

Name heights x widths:
Dasher: 1⅛" x 4⅛"
Dancer: 1⅛" x 4"
Prancer: 1⅛" x 4⅛"
Vixon: 1¼" x 3⅜"
Comet: 1¼" x 3⅝"
Cupid: 1¾" x 3⅝"
Donner: 1⅛" x 4⅛"
Blitzen: 1½" x 3¾"

Follow General Directions to assemble name tags. Use reverse appliqué to create the black bell openings/slits.

Satin stitch reindeer names to completed name tags.

CREATE 16 JINGLE BELLS EACH:

APPLIQUÉ PIECE	COLOR	PIECE SIZE
1	Light gray/silver	3" x 3"
2	Medium gray	2" x 3"
3	Dark gray/black	2" x 2"

Follow General Directions to assemble bells, except reverse appliqué black openings. Place, glue, and stitch completed appliqués. Remove excess background fabric.

Make the bows following the General Directions. Add to completed name tags before adding the bells.

Cut away excess background fabric behind name tags, bows, and bells to within ¼" of seam lines. Attach completed appliqués to red/gold ironwork (background). See page 34–37.

Reindeer Tag

Enlarge 200%
Actual Size 7" x 6½"

Reindeer Names

Shown at 100%

Holly Vine

Appliqué Piece	Color	Piece Size
Yardage is dependent on the number and color of pieces along the vine.		
Stem	Brown or dark orange	Varies
Holly	Variety of greens	Varies
Berries	Variety of reds	Varies
Tear drop	Orange or copper	Varies

Stem (or swag vine) is cut actual pattern size. Glue along the top of the quilt to fill available spaces. It should appear to be running gracefully across the top, dropping down in areas as space allows. Enlarge, decrease, or reverse the pattern to create a variety of leaves.

Using a blanket or satin stitch, cover the entire fabric stem with thread. Variegated thread creates an attractive vine.

Cut holly leaves exact pattern size. Satin stitch into place.

Berries may be cut using raw-edge or freezer paper techniques.

After stem is placed, glued into position and stitched, add holly leaves, tear drop shapes, and all berries. Cut tear drops using raw-edge technique.

Quilt holly leaf vein lines.

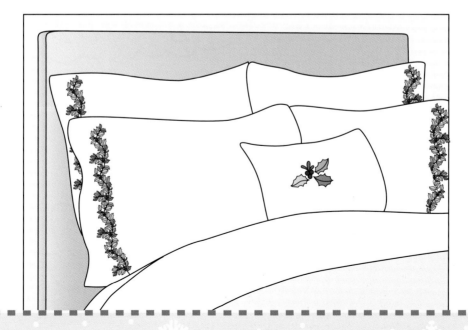

Holly Vine

Shown at 100%

ELVES

Order of Assembly

You can assemble the elves in any order and set them aside; they are presented here in alphabetical order. All of the elves are added to the quilt at the same time except the two elves on top of the sleigh. Create the two packages on the floor when you create the elves, as they will be added at the same time you add the elves.

Note:

Pattern measurements are for finished appliqué sizes.

Elf Holding Airplane

Appliqué Piece	Color	Piece Size
Elf		
1, 8, 13	Medium green	7" x 8"
2, 7, 12	Red	10" x 12"
3	Black	2" x 4"
4, 5, 6, 10, 11	Gold	5" x 6"
9	Flesh color	4" x 5"
14, 15	White	4" x 5"
Eyes	White	1" x 2"
	Black	1" x 1"
Mouth	Red	1" x 2"
Airplane		
1	Dark orange	2" x 2"
2	Dark red	1" x 1'
3	Light red	4" x 6"
4, 10, 11, 12, 13	White	4" x 4"
5, 6	Light orange	3" x 4"
7, 8, 9	Black	2" x 2"

Elf

Follow General Directions to assemble elf except pieces 4, 5, 6, 10, and 11. Satin stitch buckle (oval) and two circles using decorative thread. Do the same for hair.

Cut and glue white oval for eyes into place. Glue black sections on top of white. Glue mouth into place and add tooth.

Satin stitch all portions of eyes using matching thread colors. Using a free-motion technique, straight stitch around eyes and mouth three times, following the same stitching line. Cheeks, nose, and outside lines of eyes can be stitched during this process.

Satin stitch hair, tooth, and mouth using matching thread color.

Airplane

Follow General Directions to assemble airplane except pieces 4, 10, 11, 12, and 13; also pieces 7, 8, and 9 (propeller). Satin stitch using matching threads. Pieces 7, 8, and 9 will be satin stitched after entire appliqué is completed, placed, and glued onto background fabric. Place stabilizer behind pieces 10, 11, 12, and 13. Satin stitch narrowly using matching thread color.

Position and glue pieces in numerical order. Hand stitch the balance of airplane and wings using matching thread colors. Set aside.

Position, glue, and stitch airplane to elf arm.

Place and glue completed appliqué to background under top left seat of airplane.

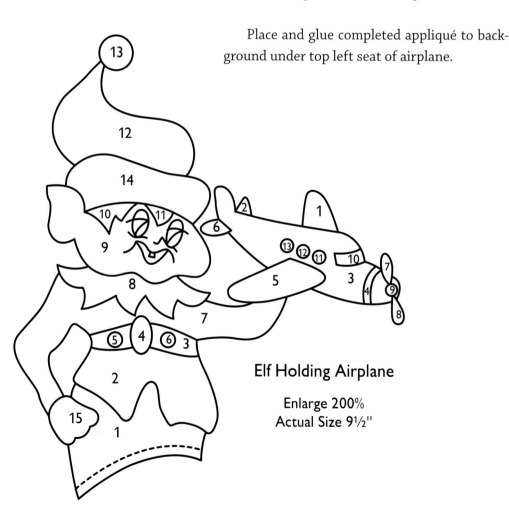

Elf Holding Airplane

Enlarge 200%
Actual Size 9½"

Elf with Basketball

Appliqué Piece	Color	Piece Size
Elf		
A	Gray tone of background color	4" x 6"
1, 5, 8, 9	Light green	14" x 14"
2	Dark green	10" x 10"
4, 7, 11, 13	Red	6" x 8"
3, 6, 10, 12, 14, 17	White	9" x 12"
15, 18	Flesh	6" x 6"
16	Yellow or red	1" x 1"
Eyes	White	1" x 2"
	Blue	1" x 2"
	Tan	1" x 1"
Nose	Medium to dark pink	1" x 1"
Mouth	Medium pink	2" x 2"
Basketball		
1, 3	Rust	4" x 4"
2, 4, 5	Brown	4" x 5"
6, 7	Dark rust	4" x 4"

Elf

Body and legs (piece 1) are cut as one piece, adding ¼" seam allowance around template. No need to iron down seams at this time. Cut all dark green pieces (piece 2) adding ¼" seam allowances only to outside (short) sides. Place light green (piece 1) on master pattern; glue all dark green (piece 2) sections to piece 1. Satin stitch all pieces (2). Press, then reposition template on back side of fabric. Iron seam allowances towards freezer paper, clipping when necessary. Remove template and pin to master pattern.

Turn under pieces 3, 4, 6, and 7. Create circles 5 and 8. Glue all pieces to body. Make all upper body pieces; glue in place.

Satin stitch narrowly around both sections of eyes, nose and mouth. Use a thread color that contrasts with face color. Free-motion straight stitch around features three times, following the same stitching line.

Place, glue, and hand stitch elf to background, leaving hand/cuff area free.

Basketball

Cut pieces 2, 4, and 5, adding ⅛" to long sides and ¼" to short sides. Prepare templates for 1, 3, 6, and 7, ironing under all inside seams. Place and glue all sections in place. Hand or machine piece together. Make template for entire ball. Center freezer paper and, with wetting solution, iron outside edges toward template. Remove freezer paper and set aside.

Place and glue completed basketball under the elf hand/cuff area but over the chest area. Stitch basketball to elf and stitch hand/cuff area to basketball.

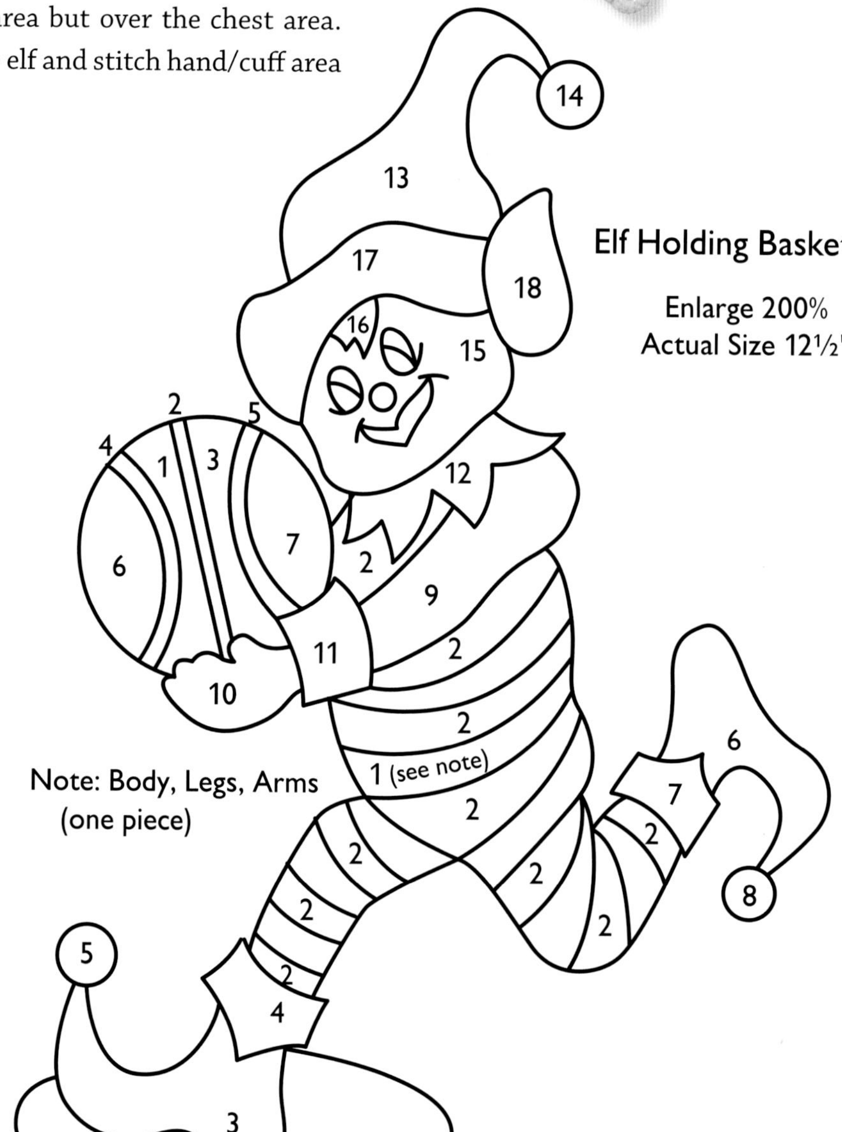

Elf Holding Basketball

Enlarge 200%
Actual Size 12½"

Note: Body, Legs, Arms
(one piece)

Elf Behind Toy Bag

Appliqué Piece	Color	Piece Size
Elf		
1, 10	Red	6" x 6"
2, 3, 11	Medium green	7" x 7"
4, 7, 12	White	6" x 6"
5	Gold	3" x 4"
6	White (buckle)	2" x 2"
8, 13	Flesh	4" x 5"
9	Brown	2" x 2"
Eyes	White and black	1" x 1" each
Mouth	White and brown	1" x 1" each
Package		
1, 3	White	3" x 4"
2, 8, 9, 12	Yellow	5" x 5"
4, 6	Ivory	3" x 3"
5, 7, 11	Gold	4" x 4"
10	Dark yellow	2" x 2"

Elf

Follow General Directions to assemble elf except buckle (piece 6). Cut buckle exact pattern size and glue into place. Satin stitch wide enough to cover entire fabric ring using decorative thread.

Cut and glue eyes, hair, and mouth exact shape of patterns. Satin stitch all areas using matching threads. Using black thread, free-motion straight stitch around eyes and mouth three times, following the same stitching lines. This stitching line also forms the smile lines at eyes and mouth.

Package

Assemble package following General Directions. Pieces 1, 2, 3, 4, 5, and 6 may be machine or hand pieced. Stitch all seams using matching threads.

Place and glue completed package to elf arm; stitch, joining seam.

Position, glue, and stitch elf/package appliqué to background fabric.

Gift: numbers 1–12

Elf: number 1–13

Elf Behind Bag

Enlarge 200%
Actual Size 9¾"

(under bag)

Elf with Cowboy Hat

APPLIQUÉ PIECE	COLOR	PIECE SIZE
Elf		
1, 9, 13	Red	12" x 13"
2, 3, 6	Black	6" x 6"
7	Gold	2" x 2"
4, 5, 14, 15	Medium green	6" x 6"
8	Light green	3" x 5"
10, 11, 12	Flesh	4" x 5"
Eyes	White and black	1" x 1" each
Mouth	White and black	1" x 1" each
Cowboy Hat		
16	Dark tan	5" x 5"
17	Light tan	3" x 3"
18	Medium tan	3" x 3"
19	Gold	2" x 2"

Elf

Follow General Directions to assemble elf and hat except buckle. Cut buckle fabric exact pattern; glue into place. Place stabilizer behind buckle and satin stitch with decorative threads. Set the width of the stitch to cover entire buckle fabric. Stitch slowly around corners and adjust stitch width for best results.

Cut white for eyes; glue into place. Glue black sections into place on white fabric. Cut black mouth section; glue into place. Add white teeth onto mouth and glue. Narrowly satin stitch all areas using matching threads. Using a free-motion straight stitch technique and black thread, stitch around all features three times, following the same stitching line. Note that the nose and cheeks are formed at this time.

Hat

Cut star actual size and satin stitch it with decorative threads. Consider crystals for embellishment. Make ties of couched yarn or cording. Use a bead for the hat slide.

Place and glue completed appliqué on background.

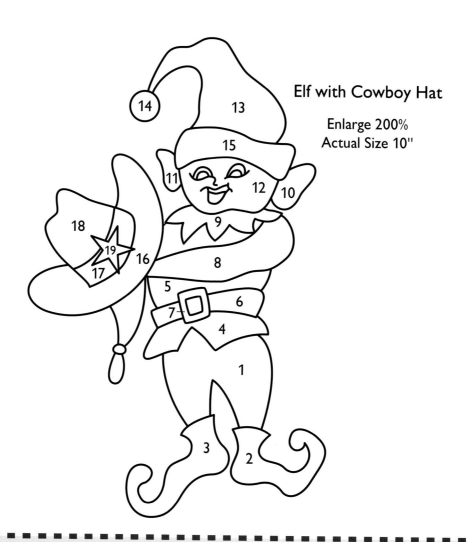

Elf with Cowboy Hat

Enlarge 200%
Actual Size 10"

Elf with Doll

Appliqué Piece	Color	Piece Size
Elf		
A	Gray tone of background color	4" x 6"
1, 9, 11	Red	11" x 14"
2, 4, 6, 8, 12, 14	Yellow/gold	8" x 10"
3, 5	Dark gold	6" x 8"
7	Dark yellow	3" x 4"
10, 13,	Flesh	4" x 4"
Eyes	White	1" x 2"
	Black	1" x 1"
Mouth and nose	Coral	2" x 2"
Doll		
15, 20, 29	Dark blue	6" x 7"
16, 19, 25, 28	Pink	4" x 4"
18, 22, 23	Medium blue	6" x 8"
21	Light blue	3" x 5"
17, 24, 26	Flesh	2" x 3"
27	Yellow/gold	1" x 1"
Eyes	White and blue	1" x 1" each

Follow General Directions to assemble elf/doll unit. Cut doll hair and pink collar exact pattern size; narrowly satin stitch.

Use a free-motion stitching technique to straight stitch around all eyes three times, following the same stitching line.

Place, glue, and stitch appliqué onto background fabric.

Elf with Doll

Elf with Doll

Enlarge 200%
Actual Size 9¼"

Elf with Gift (on Steps)

APPLIQUÉ PIECE	COLOR	PIECE SIZE
Elf		
A	Gray tone of background fabric	3" x 5"
1, 2, 17	Flesh color	4" x 6"
3, 5, 18	Red	6" x 6"
4, 6, 7, 8	Medium green	6" x 6"
9, 10, 11, 19, 20	White	6" x 6"
Eyes	White and black	1" x 1" each
Mouth and nose	Red	1" x 2"
Gift		
12, 14, 16	Gold	4" x 6"
13, 15	White	2" x 2"

Follow General Directions to assemble elf and gift. Package pieces 12, 13, 14, 15, and 16 may be machine pieced together before turning under all outside seam allowances. Add green stitching lines on bow during quilting.

Cut and place white and black eye pieces, nose, and mouth. Satin stitch narrowly around all features using matching threads. Using black thread, free-motion straight stitch around eyes three times, following previously sewn lines.

Elf with Gift (on steps)

Enlarge 200%
Actual Size 8¾"

Elf with Packages and Ice Skates

Elf

Appliqué Piece	Color	Piece Size
Elf		
A	Gray tone of background fabric	3" x 7"
1, 12, 17, 20, 25	Red	16" x 18"
2, 3, 9	Black	9" x 14"
4, 5, 6, 7, 16, 26	Dark green	10" x 10"
8, 11, 27	Medium green	10" x 14"
21, 23, 24	Flesh	4" x 5"
13, 14, 15, 18, 19, 22	White	8" x 8"
10	Copper (buckle and straps)	2" x 2"
Eyes	White	2" x 2"
	Black and tan	1" x 1" each
Nose	Tan	1" x 1"

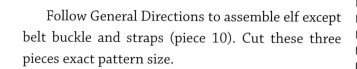

Follow General Directions to assemble elf except belt buckle and straps (piece 10). Cut these three pieces exact pattern size.

Place and glue copper belt buckle and straps. Using matching thread, cover entire width of fabric with satin stitch. Walk the needle around the rounded corners to achieve a smooth appearance.

Cut entire eye of white fabric; add and glue black and tan pieces. Glue nose in place. Narrowly stitch each piece using a satin stitch and matching threads. Using black thread, free-motion straight stitch around the eyes three times, following the same stitching line.

Elf with Stack of Packages

Enlarge 200%
Actual Size 13"

Packages

Appliqué Piece	Color	Piece Size
STACK OF PACKAGES		
Package A		
A1, A2, A3	White	8" x 9"
A4, A7, A9, A12	Medium red	4" x 5"
A5, A6, A8, A10, A11	Dark red	6" x 6"
Package B		
B1, B5	Dark red	6" x 6"
B2, B4	Light red	4" x 6"
B3, B6, B7, B9, B10, B11, B13	Light green	5" x 6"
B8, B12, B14	Dark green	4" x 4"
Package C		
C1	Dark green	3" x 5"
C2, C4,	Light green	3" x 5"
C5, C7	Medium green	3" x 5"
C3, C6, C8, C9, C14	Dark gold	6" x 6"
C12, C13	Medium yellow	3" x 4"
C10, C11	Light yellow	2" x 4"
Package D		
D1	Dark blue	3" x 3"
D5, D7	Medium blue	3" x 5"
D2, D4	Light blue	4" x 4"
D3, D6	White	3" x 4"
D8	Medium green	2" x 2"
D9	Dark green	2" x 2"
D10	Light green	2" x 2"
D11, D12, D13	Red	3" x 3"

Follow General Directions to assemble each package individually. Position and pin each package. Glue packages together. Hand stitch glued seam lines using matching threads.

Place tear-away stabilizer only behind package D. Satin stitch holly using decorative threads. To achieve ribbon curls, glue cording into place and allow to dry. Using decorative thread, select a zigzag stitch width just to cover the cording. Stitch slowly following cording. Stitch berries using matching or decorative threads with a narrow satin stitch.

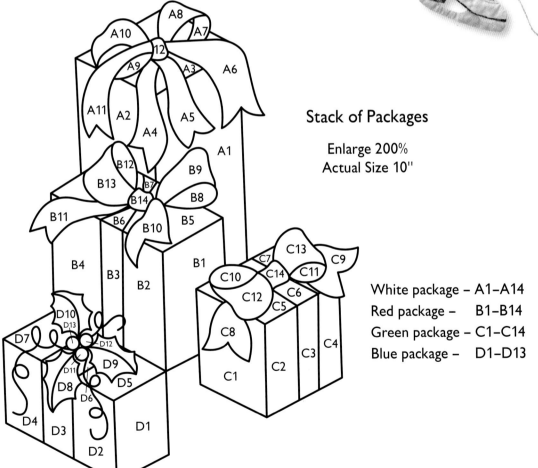

Stack of Packages

Enlarge 200%
Actual Size 10"

White package – A1–A14
Red package –   B1–B14
Green package – C1–C14
Blue package –   D1–D13

Ice Skates

Appliqué Piece	Color	Piece Size
Ice Skates		
1	Gray or silver	5" x 5"
2	Brown	4" x 4"
3	White	8" x 8"
4	Tan	2" x 4"
5	Light tan	4" x 6"
6	White	4" x 4"
	OR	
	White cording	16"

Follow General Directions to assemble ice skates.

Construct two entire skates so that arrangement may be adjusted. Place, glue, and hand stitch completed appliqué onto background fabric.

EYELETS

Choose one of two construction methods:

1 Glue fabric circles on skates. Narrowly satin stitch using a slightly darker thread color.

2 Mark circles on piece 5 with a water-soluble marker. Place tear-away stabilizer under area to be stitched. Select a satin stitch width ½ the size of the circle. Walk the stitching around the circle noting that each stitch will be placed in the center hole (center of eyelet). This requires a bit of time and patience, but the results are worth the effort.

LACES

Stitch laces after the skate appliqué is attached to the background fabric. Choose one of two construction methods:

1 Cut laces from white fabric; place and glue into position. Satin stitch narrowly to just cover the fabric width; this may need adjusting as fabric narrows.

2 Glue any type of narrow round cording directly onto completed skates and use a zigzag width to cover edges of cording. Backtrack two stitches at end of cording.

Place and glue completed appliqué on background.

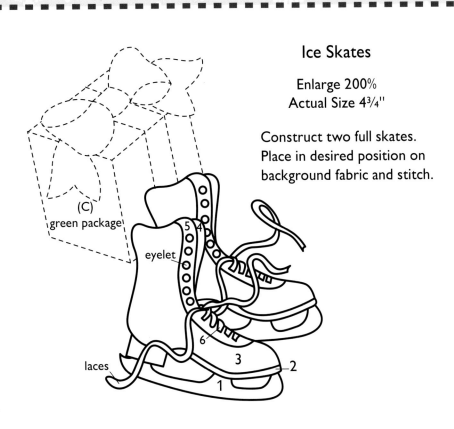

Ice Skates

Enlarge 200%
Actual Size 4¾"

Construct two full skates.
Place in desired position on
background fabric and stitch.

(C)
green package

5 4

eyelet

6

3

2

laces

1

Elf Holding Pink Package

Appliqué Piece	Color	Piece Size
Elf		
A	Gray tone of background fabric	3" x 7"
1, 2, 20	Black	8" x 8"
3 (pants), 16, 18, 21	Red	10" x 10"
4, 5, 6, 7, 8, 9, 10, 15	Light green	10" x 10"
13, 17	Medium green	12" x 12"
11, 12, 14	White	7" x 7"
19	Flesh	6" x 6"
Eyes	White	2" x 2"
	Black	1" x 1"
Nose	Black	1" x 1"
Mouth	Medium pink	2" x 2"
Package		
1, 3, 5	Very light pink	3" x 3"
2, 4, 6, 7	Dark pink	8" x 9"
8, 10, 11	Medium pink	4" x 4"
9	Light pink	5" x 5"

Elf

Follow General Directions to assemble elf except pants. Cut red pants adding ¼" seam allowance around entire template. Cut all light green stripes adding ¼" allowances only to outside narrow edges. Satin stitch stripes to red pants excluding short outside edges. Leave sections under cuffs and jacket open; these are seam allowances that will be placed under pieces 11, 12, and 13.

Cut and glue white circles for eyes and glue black section in place. Place and glue nose and mouth into place. Satin stitch all features using matching threads. Using black thread, free-motion straight stitch around eyes and mouth three times, following the same stitching line. All smile lines can be stitched at this time.

Package

Place and glue the package to the completed elf; stitch, joining seams.

Place and glue the completed appliqué to background.

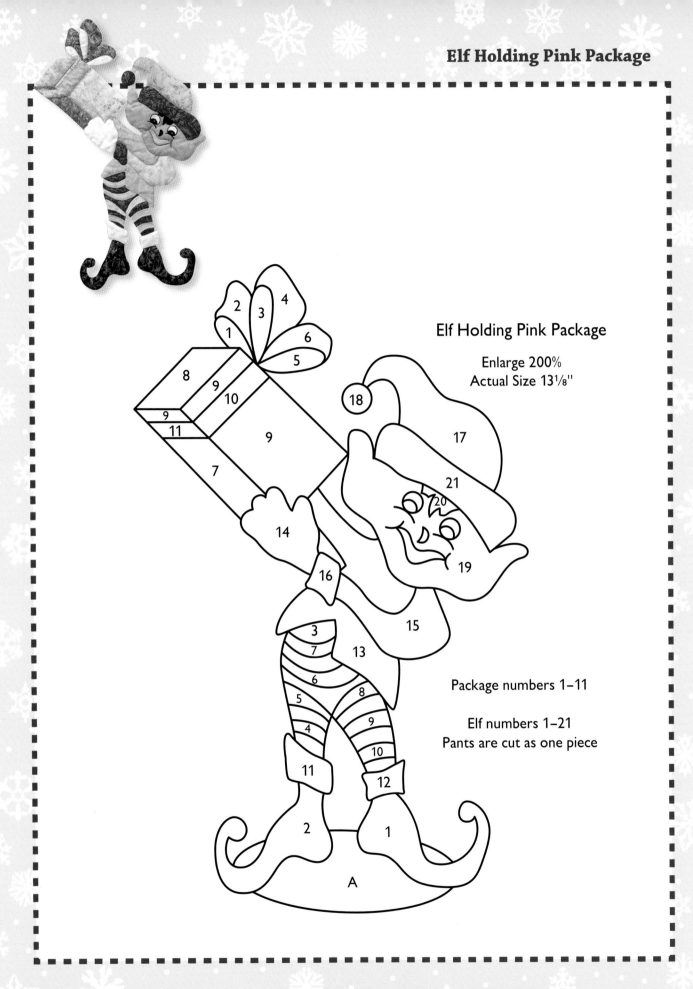

Elf Holding Pink Package

Enlarge 200%
Actual Size 13⅛"

Package numbers 1–11

Elf numbers 1–21
Pants are cut as one piece

Elf on Rocking Horse

Appliqué Piece	Color	Piece Size
Elf		
1	Black	2" x 3"
2, 5, 8, 9, 10, 11, 14	Red	9" x 14"
3, 6, 15	White	4" x 6"
4, 7, 12	Medium green	6" x 6"
13	Flesh	4" x 5"
Eyes	White	1" x 1"
	Green	1" x 1"
Horse		
5	Gray	12" x 12"
1, 2, 26, 28, 29, 30	Black	5" x 6"
3, 19, 21, 23, 25	Ivory or cream	7" x 7"
4, 20, 22, 24, 27	White	7" x 7"
6, 11	Red	2" x 4"
7, 9, 13, 14	Rust	5" x 7"
8, 18	Yellow	4" x 4"
10, 12, 16, 17	Blue	7" x 10"
15	Gold	1" x 1"
Rocker		
1	Medium green	4" x 9"
2, 3, 4, 5, 6	Red	4" x 5"
7, 8, 10, 11	Same color as background	3" x 4"
9	Light green	5" x 10"
A	Gray tone of background fabric	3" x 6"

Elf

Follow General Directions to assemble elf. For eyes, cut full white sections. Glue black sections on top of white pieces. Glue eyes, nose, and mouth pieces. Narrowly satin stitch all face pieces using matching thread colors. Free-motion stitch around eyes three times, following the same stitching line. Set aside.

Horse

Follow General Directions to assemble horse, except draw pattern for pieces 8 and 10 as if elf leg and foot were not present. Tassels can be created with free-motion quilting. When stitching piece 15, select a satin stitch width to cover the entire fabric using matching color thread. Glue completed horse to rocker.

Rocker

Follow General Directions to assemble rocker. Cut rocker pieces 1 and 9 each as one piece. Glue and stitch prepared pieces 2, 3, 4, 5, and 6 onto section. Add 7 and 8 to piece 1. Add front rocker pieces 9, 10, and 11. Glue rocker onto piece A.

Place, glue, and stitch elf onto horse. Place and glue the completed appliqué to background.

Elf on Rocking Horse

Enlarge 200%
Actual Size 12¼"

Elf with Scroll (Includes Alphabet)

Appliqué Piece	Color	Piece Size
Elf		
A	Darker value of background	5" x 8"
1, 10, 11	Dark red	7" x 7"
2, 4, 9	Medium green	4" x 5"
3, 7	Black	5" x 8"
5, 8, 13, 20	Red	12" x 12"
6	Light green	5" x 6"
12, 14, 15, 21, 22	White	10" x 10"
16	Light gold	3" x 3"
17, 19	Flesh	4" x 6"
18	Light gray or white	4" x 6"
23	Dark gold	1" x 2"
Eye	White and blue	1" x 1" each
Glasses	Pearlized crinkle sheer iridescent film	3" x 3"
Scroll		
B	Medium tan	3" x 4"
C	Medium dark tan	2" x 3"
D, F	Dark tan	12" x 13"
E	Light tan	6" x 12"
Alphabet	Red embroidery thread	2 strands

Elf

Follow General Directions to assemble elf appliqué.

EYE AND MOUTH

Cut white circle actual pattern size. Glue blue pupil into place. Glue entire eye to face. Stitch blue area with a narrow satin stitch; stitch remaining white area. Sew around entire eye with dark color thread twice to add depth. Free-motion stitch mouth and circle on cheek in red.

GLASSES

Apply Steam-A-Seam Lite to back of 2 squares of iridescent film. Use a pressing cloth when applying medium heat to this fabric.

Cut out oval and adhere to elf face, placing one lens on top of face and one lens under nose (add seam allowance). After placing stitched appliqué onto background fabric, stitch the lens with gold metallic thread using a medium width and length setting. A tight satin stitch will cut this delicate film fabric, so use a more open setting. Make a sample to determine machine settings.

Scroll

Follow General Directions to assemble scroll. Set aside.

Draw scroll design on paper, including dotted lines for name placement. Write desired names on paper lines with fine-tip black marker. Connect all letters where necessary. Place fabric over the drawn scroll section and trace names onto fabric using a water-soluble blue marker. Place lightweight tear-away stabilizer under scroll fabric. Use alphabet patterns or free-motion stitch names using machine embroidery hoop or hand embroidery. Follow stitching lines for each name when quilting; double stitching will add depth of color to this area.

Alphabet

Choose one of two options to place names on scroll:

1 Draw scroll design on paper, including dotted lines for name placement. Write names on paper lines with a fine-tip black marker. Connect all letters where necessary. Place fabric over the inked scroll and trace names using a water-soluble blue marker. Place lightweight stabilizer under scroll fabric. Use alphabet patterns or free-motion stitch names using machine embroidery hoop, or hand stitch. Follow stitching lines when quilting; double stitching will add depth.

2 Hand embroider your favorite names using 2 strands of embroidery floss.

Place and glue completed scroll appliqué to elf and lower oval A. Stitch glued connecting areas.

Pen

Cut piece 16 exact pattern size; add piece 23 on top. Narrowly satin stitch after entire appliqué is completed.

Position, glue, and stitch completed elf/scroll/pen appliqué onto background.

Elf with Scroll (Includes Alphabet)

abcdefghijklmnopqrstuvwxyz
ABCDEFGHIJKLMNO
PQRSTUVWXYZ *Alphabet Actual Size*

Enlarge 200%
Actual Size 12¾"

Vein of feather is satin stitched

Raw-edge feather has
medium width satin
stitch finish

Elf with Teddy Bear

Appliqué Piece	Color	Piece Size
Elf		
A	Gray tone of background fabric	3" x 6"
1, 2, 7, 11, 21	Gold	12" x 16"
5, 6, 8, 9, 13, 18	Red	10" x 14"
3, 4	Dark green	5" x 8"
10, 14, 15, 19	Medium green	6" x 8"
12	Light green	2" x 2"
16, 17, 20	Flesh	6" x 6"
Eyes	White and blue	1" x 1" each
Mouth	Tan and pink	1" x 1" each
Teddy Bear		
1, 2, 5, 9, 15	Medium blue	8" x 8"
3, 4, 10, 11, 13	Dark blue	3" x 3"
6, 12, 14, 16	Light blue	4" x 5"
21, 23	Light yellow	2" x 2"
25	Medium yellow	1" x 1"
19, 20, 22, 24	Dark yellow	3" x 3"
7, 8 (circles on tummy)	Medium yellow	1" x 1"
17, 18 (eyes)	Brown	1" x 1'
Nose	Black	1" x 1"
Eyes	Black	2" x 2"

Elf

Follow General Directions to assemble elf except circle 14; glue into place last.

For mouth, cut the inside tan piece the size of the full mouth, then glue pink upper and lower lip on top of it.

Narrowly satin stitch all areas. Using free-motion stitching technique, stitch around eyes three times, following the same stitching line. Smile lines are stitched at this time.

Glue teddy bear into place. The elf back arm (piece 7) is placed under bear piece 5; elf hand (piece 12) is placed on top of bear piece 5. Hand stitch these connecting seam areas.

Teddy Bear

Follow General Directions to assemble bear except pieces 7 and 8 and eye pieces 17 and 18. Add black sections of eyes on top of pieces 17 and 18.

Narrowly satin stitch around nose, beginning where smile lines connect. Change machine to a straight stitch setting and continue stitching smile two times, following the same stitching line. Satin stitch both brown and black colors of eyes. Satin stitch pieces 7 and 8 using matching thread color.

Place and glue completed appliqué onto background fabric.

Elf with Teddy Bear

Enlarge 200%
Actual Size 8¼"

Two Packages

Appliqué Piece	Color	Piece Size
Pink and white package		
1	Light pink	3" x 3"
2	Dark pink	3" x 3"
3	Medium pink	3" x 4"
4, 5, 8, 9, 10	White	3" x 4"
6, 7	Ivory	3" x 4"
Gold package		
1	Light gold	4" x 5"
2	Medium gold	3" x 4"
3	Dark gold	4" x 5"
4, 5	White	4" x 4"
6, 7, 8, 9, 12	Light green	4" x 4"
10, 11	Dark green	3" x 3"

Follow General Directions to assemble both packages.

Place, glue, and stitch competed appliqués onto background fabric. Trim excess background fabric to within ¼" of seam line.

Two Packages

Pink and White Package

Shown at 100%
Actual Size 3"

Gold Package

Shown at 100%
Actual Size 4"

Santa's Loading Dock QUILT ❄ MARY BUVIA

SLEIGH AND TOY BAG

Order of Assembly

Sleigh

Appliqué Piece	Color	Piece Size
Sleigh Body		
1	Light yellow (top back sleigh)	24" x 27"
2	Medium gold (railing)	18" x 30"
3	Light yellow (bottom wheel)	9" x 9"
	Medium gold (inside shadow)	4" x 4"
	Dark gold (inside background)	4" x 4"
4	Light green (lower left sleigh)	9" x 16"
5	Medium green	8" x 16"
6	Dark green	6" x 6"
7	Red (tufted upper left back)	10" x 10"
8	Medium gold (lower connecting bar)	8" x 46"
9	Copper	9" x 18"
10	Light red	5" x 5"
11	Medium red	4" x 5"
12, 13	Dark red	4" x 9"
Inside Railing Trim	Medium gold	15" x 40"
Posts and Balls	Light gold	12" x 18"
Candy Canes	White	10" x 20"
	Green	10" x 20"
Tufted Chair		
Back and seat (solid piece)	Medium red	13" x 17"
(pieced sections)		20" x 20"
Arms	Light red	9" x 9"
Front Arm Trim	Copper	8" x 8"

Sleigh continues on page 77.

Sleigh – continued

Appliqué Piece	Color	Piece Size
Curved Lower Trim Sections of Chair		
A	Medium tan	3" x 7"
B	Medium beige	3" x 7"
C	Light beige	4" x 7"
D	Medium beige	3" x 7"
E	Medium tan	4" x 6"
F	Dark tan	4" x 6"
G	Medium brown	3" x 5"
H	Dark brown	3" x 5"
Trim Above Floor Board	Copper	5" x 8"
Floor		
I	Light beige	1" x 5"
J	Medium beige	1" x 5"
K	Medium tan	1" x 4"
L	Dark tan	1" x 4"
M	Medium brown	1" x 3"
Wood Chair Back Frame		
Front	Copper	13" x 13"
Left shadow	Medium brown	6" x 13"
14	Light tan	18" x 20"
15	Light brown	4" x 14"
16	Dark tan	5" x 7"
Back Runner		
17	Dark yellow	14" x 63"
Shadow areas	Dark gold	12" x 60"
Front Runner		
18	Light yellow	16" x 66"
Shadow areas	Medium gold	16" x 66"

Follow General Directions to assemble sleigh except cut sleigh runners, side railing, and back exact pattern size. Satin stitch using matching or decorative threads.

Follow this cutting and placement order for sleigh. Add seam allowances where needed for some appliqué pieces:

1 Cut top and back section (piece 1). Note that this area extends under the entire back section of railing only. Cut and add all parts of piece 2. Add all parts of pieces 3, 4, 5, and 6. Place and glue ornamentations (see pages 86–87). Add back section of railing.

2 Cut and place front four sections of inside railings. Glue all posts in place. Cut, place, and glue all circles in place on top of posts. Add seam allowances in those areas where inside railings are placed under posts.

3 Add completed "Santa" letters. Glue all areas that touch railings and posts.

4 Cut and glue red tufted area (piece 7) on upper back of sleigh/toy bag. Add seam allowances where it is placed under upper back of sleigh.

5 Add completed toy bag and ribbon (see pages 80–81). The bag will be visible under only the first four sections of railing. Glue areas touching bag including all inside railings.

6 Cut, place, and glue connecting bar (piece 8). At this time, all satin stitching may be completed using matching or decorative threads.

7 Prepare pieces 9, 10, 11, 12, and 13 (Santa's chair) following General Directions. Place and glue.

⑧ Cut entire candy canes using white fabric. Cut all green sections and glue into place on top of white fabric. Red stitching lines on white fabric may be added after green sections are stitched or during the quilting process. Place and glue completed candy canes onto back of chair.

⑨ Red tufted seat and back may be constructed by drawing the tufted lines on a solid piece of red fabric and stitching them during the quilting process. Another option is to hand piece all sections together. Stitch in the ditch during the quilting process. Place front arm sections (copper) onto top arm sections. Dotted lines indicate quilting lines. Place and glue onto seat and back of chair.

⑩ Cut wood frame for top of chair and add left side shadowing (medium brown). Glue into place.

⑪ Beginning with A, place and glue pieces through H. It will be necessary to cut and place a piece of dark brown to close up small gaps under curved areas.

⑫ Piece together floor board sections I through M, allowing seam allowances to tuck under front of sleigh and be joined with curved pieces A through H. Match same color seam lines where these sections are stitched together.

⑬ Piece 14, sleigh front, may be cut exact pattern size (raw-edge) or use freezer paper technique (see General Directions). Place, pin, and glue into place where it joins other appliqué pieces. If satin-stitching, do this after entire sleigh and toy bag appliqué is placed on background fabric. Add completed sleigh bell (see page 90) at hanging position on piece 14.

⑭ Cut pieces 15 and 16, join at short seam line, and place into position at bottom of chair.

⑮ Cut all pieces of back runner (piece 17). Add seam allowances where necessary on those pieces to be placed under another section. Glue all those areas that are under another section.

⑯ Cut all pieces of front runner (piece 18). Add seam allowances where necessary on those pieces to be placed under another section. Glue all those areas that are under another section.

⑰ Glue the completed front runner to the back runner. Front portion of the forward runner will be placed under 15 and left candy cane appliqué. Glue this area.

⑱ After entire sleigh, toy bag (page 84), and bow (page 84) are completed, place and glue them into desired positions on background fabric.

Note: This sleigh is designed to be placed at an angle onto quilt top; i.e., front portion of sleigh should be placed lower than back area.

Sleigh

Sleigh

Enlarge 400%
Actual Size 62$^{15}/_{16}$" x 28$^{3}/_{4}$"

See color on page 78.

Sleigh

Enlarge 400%
Actual Size 62¹⁵⁄₁₆" x 28³⁄₄"

See color on page 78.

Sleigh

Enlarge 400%
Actual Size 62^{15}/$_{16}$" x 28^{3}/$_{4}$"

See color on page 78.

Toy Bag, Jingle Bells, Bow, and Toy Placement

APPLIQUE PIECE	COLOR	PIECE SIZE
Toy Bag		
1, 3, 34	Dark brown	20" x 24"
2, 4	Light brown	16" x 24"
6, 10, 16, 22, 26, 30	Copper	24" x 36"
7, 8, 12, 14, 17, 20, 36	Medium tan	24" x 24"
11, 13, 18, 19, 37, 38	Light tan	20" x 24"
23, 24	Dark tan	10" x 14"
27, 28, 31, 32, 35	Medium brown	12" x 18"
39	Medium tan	18" x 24"
5, 9, 15, 21, 25, 29, 33	Red	18" x 18"
Jingle Bells		
See page 42		
Bow		
2, 4, 6, 9, 11	Light red	15" x 15"
3, 7, 10, 12	Medium red	12" x 15"
1, 5, 8, 13	Dark red	10" x 10"

Follow General Directions to assemble toy bag. Add bag liner (piece 39) after all toys are stitched onto it.

Place and glue completed jingle bells (see page 42). Set aside until sleigh is completed.

Place and glue bow to toy bag at pieces 1 and 13 (dotted lines). Glue pieces 1, 2, 3, 4, and 11 on top of the bag. Piece 6 may be placed under or on top of bag.

Toy Bag, Jingle Bells, Bow, and Toy Placement

Toy Bag and Bow

Enlarge 400%
Actual Size 33" x 22"
See color on page 78.

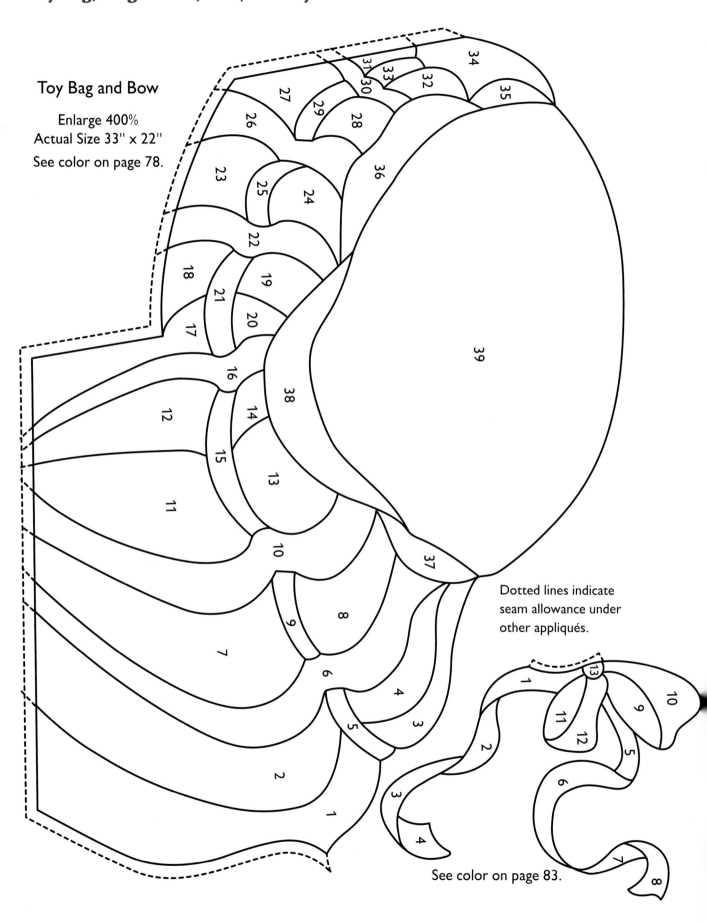

Dotted lines indicate seam allowance under other appliqués.

See color on page 83.

Toy Placement

Turn under top curved edge of piece 39 and press down seam. Arrange the toys and pin into place (see below for toy placement order). Begin with tennis racquet; toy appliqués will be placed atop one another as you work down to the panda. Take care to leave adequate seam allowances for gluing and stitching under other areas.

These toys will be inside the bag: the upper left package (19), Raggedy Ann doll (20), drum (22), panda (24), and portion of the lower right package with holly (14). Leave these areas unglued and unstitched until the lip of the bag is added. When adding the lip of the bag to the liner, notice the areas of the toys that rest on the lip, including spinning top (15) beside panda.

When all toys are in place and seam allowances are adequate, glue the outside edges in place on the bag. The bag liner with toys should appear to be a single layer of fabric. Trim away liner fabric behind each stitched toy.

1 tennis racquet
2 skis
3 football
4 Christmas tree
5 horn
6 teddy bear (upper left)
7 sailboat
8 guitar
9 crayon box
10 round ball
11 doll
12 cradle
13 teddy bear (lower right)
14 package (lower right)
15 spinning top
16 nutcracker
17 blocks
18 dog
19 package (upper left)
20 Raggedy Ann doll
21 drum sticks
22 drum
23 train
24 panda bear

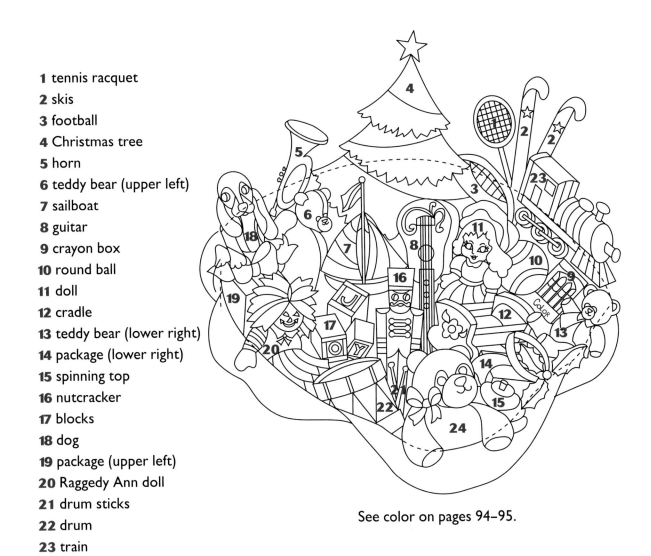

See color on pages 94–95.

Sleigh Ornamentations

APPLIQUÉ PIECE	COLOR	PIECE SIZE
Wedges		
A		
1	Light red	3" x 5"
2	Dark red	3" x 6"
B		
1	Light red	5" x 6"
2	Medium red	2" x 2"
3	Dark red	6" x 6"
C		
1	Light red	3" x 5"
2	Dark red	3" x 5"
D		
1	Light red	4" x 5"
2	Dark red	4" x 4"
Oval		
1	Light red	3" x 3"
2	Dark red	2" x 3"
3	White	2" x 2"
Stars	Medium red	3" x 5"

Follow General Directions to assemble ornamentations except for stars. Cut all stars exact pattern size. Satin stitch using decorative or matching threads.

Place and glue wedges, ovals, and stars into position.

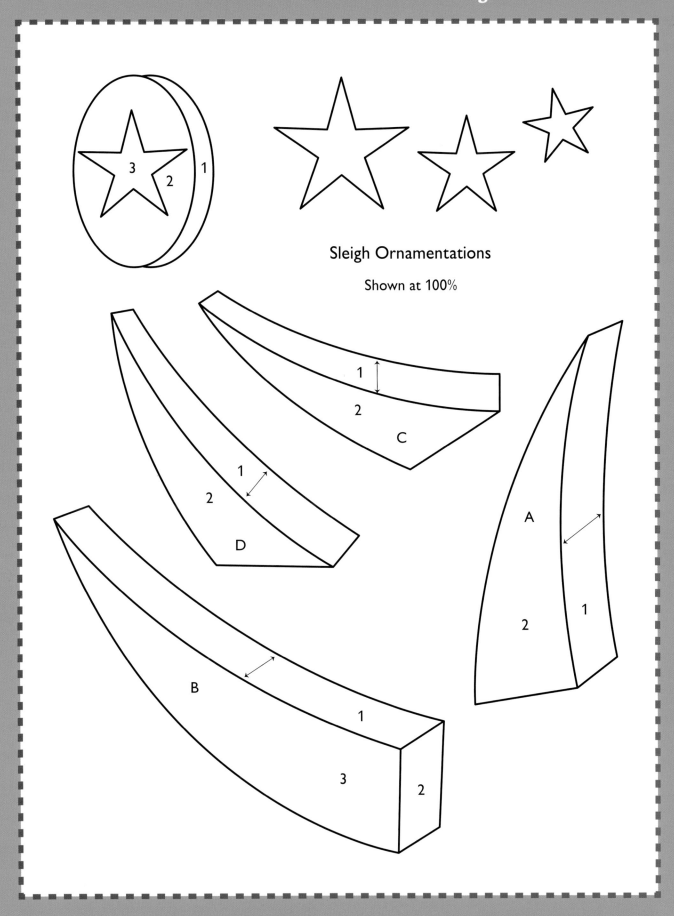

Sleigh Ornamentations

Shown at 100%

"Santa" Letters

Appliqué Piece	Color	Piece Size
Shadows (piece 1)	Green	10" x 18"
Letters (piece 2)	Red	10" x 18"

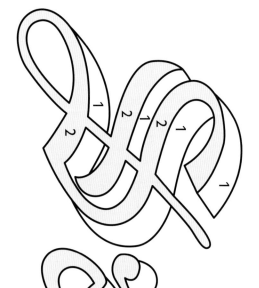

Cut green letter shadows actual size except for adding seam allowances in areas to be glued to red letters.

Cut red letters actual size. Place and glue on top of green letter shadows.

Place, glue, and stitch red/green letters on completed sleigh and toy bag.

Santa Name

Enlarge 200%
Actual Size of letter S
5" x 5"

Sleigh Lamp

Appliqué Piece	Color	Piece Size
1, 6, 8, 9	Black	6" x 8"
2, 3, 4	Copper	4" x 4"
5	Silver gray	2" x 3"
7	Light yellow	4" x 4"

Follow General Directions to assemble sleigh lamp except cut piece 1 exact pattern size; satin stitch.

Place, glue, and stitch assembled lamp onto completed Santa chair.

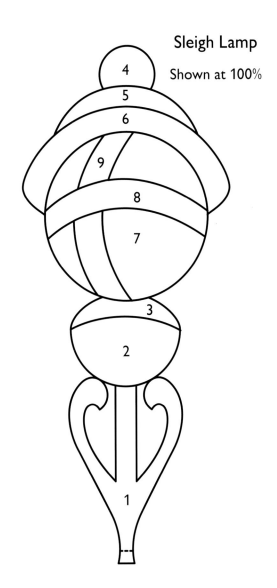

Sleigh Lamp

Shown at 100%

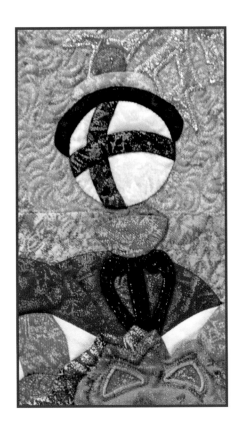

Sleigh Bell

Appliqué Piece	Color	Piece Size
A, B, C, D, E	Gold	3" x 3"
1, 3, 4, 6, 7, 10	Red	4" x 4"
2	White	3" x 4"
5	Silver	2" x 4"
8	Light green	2" x 2"
9	Medium green	2" x 2"

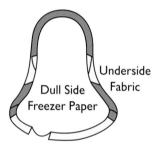

Underside Fabric

Dull Side Freezer Paper

FIG. 1

Follow General Directions to assemble bell with one exception: Do not turn under fabric edges around perimeter of bell; do that after the inside sections are sewn (pieces 1, 2, 3, 4, 5, and 6, plus pieces A, B, C, D, and E; see figure 1).

Satin stitch pieces A, B, C, D, and E to piece 2.

Glue piece 7 and bell to background; stitch. Glue pieces 8, 9, and 10 in place. Sew using a medium-wide satin stitch.

Create division lines in holly leaves with quilting lines using a light color green thread.

Add bell to completed sleigh.

Sleigh Bell

Shown at 100%

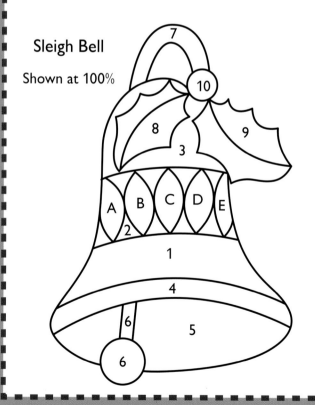

Sleigh Horn

APPLIQUÉ PIECE	COLOR	PIECE SIZE
1, 2, 5	Copper	5" x 5"
3	Gold	4" x 4"
4	Red	3" x 4"
6	Light yellow	3" x 3"

Follow General Directions to assemble sleigh horn. Leave pieces 2 and 3 open at bottom so they may be placed under the horn holder on the completed sleigh.

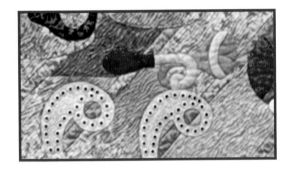

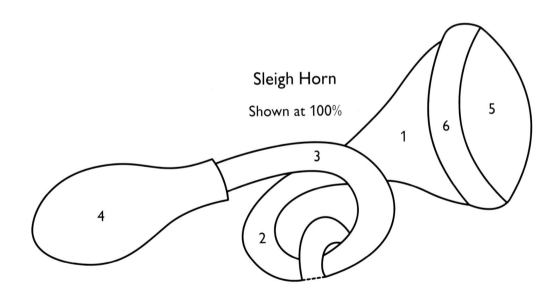

Sleigh Horn

Shown at 100%

Santa Quilting Design

Mark the quilting design in the section behind Santa's chair on the sleigh.

I machine quilted with 50-wt. Superior Threads Tiara silk thread in white; you might go heavier or lighter in your thread choice. Backtracking will be necessary in some areas. Add small crystals (2 mm or 3 mm size) in eye centers.

Small, tight, background stitching (such as stippling) around the quilted Santa will enhance this design.

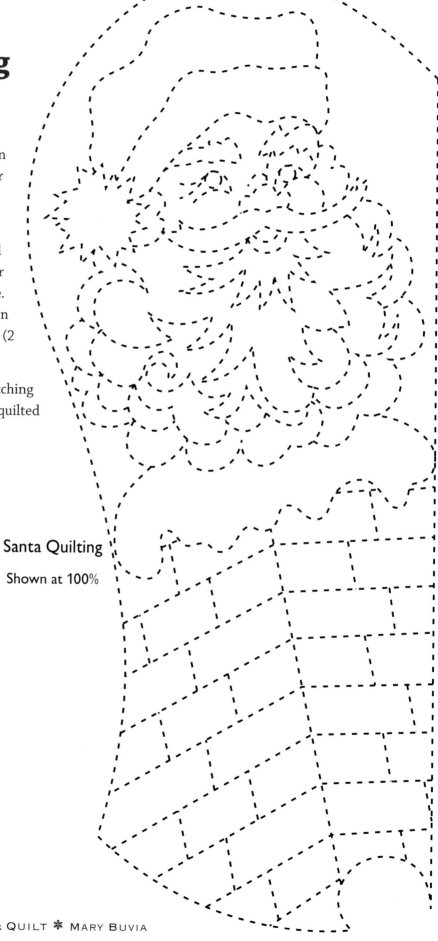

Santa Quilting

Shown at 100%

TOYS

Order of Assembly

You may create the toys in any order you like, but see page 85 for the best toy placement order. They are presented here in alphabetical order.

Follow General Directions to assemble each toy appliqué unless otherwise directed.

See page 15 for special instructions for completed toy appliqués.

Ball

Applique Piece	Color	Piece Size
1	White	4" x 5"
2, 3	Red	4" x 5"
4, 5	Navy blue	4" x 6"

Follow General Directions to assemble ball.

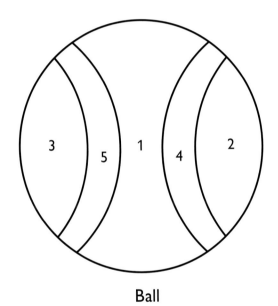

Ball

Shown at 100%

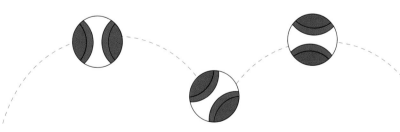

Blocks

Appliqué Piece	Color	Piece Size
Block "J"		
1	Dark purple	2" x 3"
2	Medium purple	3" x 3"
3	Medium blue	2" x 3"
4	Light purple	3" x 3"
5, 6, 7, 8	Light green	5" x 5"
Block "O"		
1	Dark blue	3" x 4"
2	Light blue	2" x 2'
3, 8	Medium blue	4" x 4"
4, 5, 6, 7	Light green	5" x 5"
Block "Y"		
1	Dark gold	2" x 2"
2	White	2" x 2"
3	Medium blue	2" x 2"
4, 5, 6, 7	Light green	5" x 5"
8	Medium yellow	2" x 3"

Blocks

Enlarge 200%

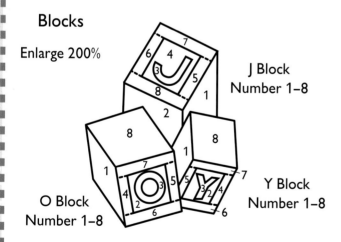

J Block
Number 1–8

O Block
Number 1–8

Y Block
Number 1–8

Piece together all block tops by hand or machine.

Cut letters exact pattern size from medium blue fabric. Place and glue on blocks. Satin stitch around all edges, or select a stitch width to cover the entire letter.

Prepare remaining pieces following General Directions. Place, glue, and stitch appliqués.

Christmas Tree

Appliqué Piece	Color	Piece Size
Tree		
1	Dark green	6" x 12"
2	Medium green	5" x 9"
3	Light green	6" x 7"
Gold cord		22"
Green cord		30"
Star		
4	White or gold	3" x 3"
Bulbs		
A	Red	3" x 6"
B	Yellow	3" x 5"
C	Blue	3" x 5"
X (bulb connectors)	Medium green	5" x 5"

Cut pieces 1, 2, and 3 exact pattern size adding ¼" seam allowances to top of pieces 1 and 2. Place, glue, and satin stitch only inside edges. Make note of satin stitch width, length, and tension; use this same setting for stitching completed appliqué in position on bag liner and background.

Place and glue cording; allow to dry. Set stitch width to just cover cording.

Place, glue, and stitch bulbs (pieces A, B, and C) and bulb connectors (piece X).

Cut star exact shape of pattern; satin stitch in place after completed tree is appliquéd to background.

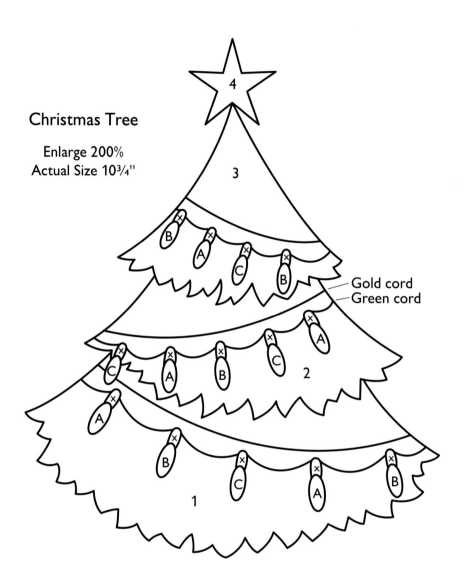

Christmas Tree

Enlarge 200%
Actual Size 10¾"

Gold cord
Green cord

Cradle

APPLIQUÉ PIECE	COLOR	PIECE SIZE
1	Medium dark green	2" x 3"
2	Medium pink	2" x 3"
3	Light pink	3" x 3"
4, 6, 7, 9, 10, 13	Medium green	8" x 8"
5, 8, 11, 12	Light green	8" x 8"
A	Yellow	2" x 2"
B	Orange	1" x 1"
C, D	Dark green	2" x 2"

Follow General Directions to assemble cradle except for pieces A, B, C, and D.

Cut pieces A, B, C and D exact pattern size. Place, glue, and stitch.

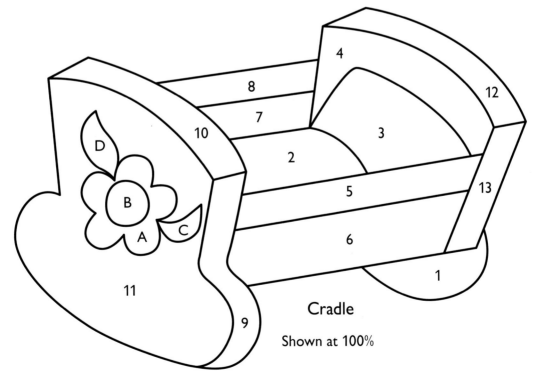

Cradle

Shown at 100%

Crayons

APPLIQUÉ PIECE	COLOR	PIECE SIZE
1	White	3" x 3"
2	Green	1" x 3"
3	Red	1" x 3"
4	Yellow	1" x 3"
5	Blue	1" x 3"
6, 7, 8, 9	Black	3" x 3"
10	Light gold	4" x 4"
11, 12	Dark gold	4" x 4"

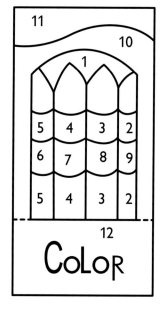

Crayons

Shown at 100%

Follow General Directions to assemble crayons with these exceptions: Cut piece 1 to include ¼" seam allowance all around. Cut crayon pieces 2 and 5 with ⅛" seam allowances on sides and ¼" seam allowances on bottom edges. Cut pieces 6 and 9 with ⅛" seam allowances on sides. These four pieces will be placed under piece 10. Cut pieces 3 and 4 with ¼" seam allowances on bottom edges but other edges exact pattern size. Satin stitch crayons to piece 1.

Place, glue, and stitch completed appliqué.

Use black stitching or black Pigma Pen to create the word "color."

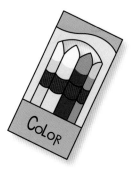

Dog

APPLIQUÉ PIECE	COLOR	PIECE SIZE
1, 4, 6, 8	Beige	6" x 6"
2, 9, 17, 18	Tan	6" x 6"
3, 5	Medium brown	4" x 4"
10, 12, 14, 15, 16	Dark brown	7" x 7"
7, 11, 13, 19, 20	Black	8" x 8"
Eyes	White	1" x 1"
	Black	1" x 1"

Follow General Directions to assemble dog except eyes.

Cut white circles for eyes, then place and glue black shape into position. Glue completed eyes onto face; satin stitch. Using free-motion technique, straight stitch around eyes at least two times, following the same stitching line with black thread.

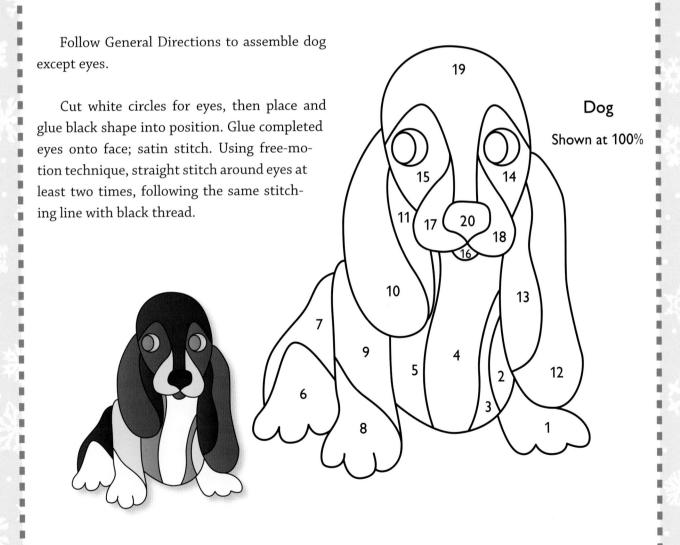

Dog
Shown at 100%

Doll

Appliqué Piece	Color	Piece Size
1, 12, 18	Flesh	5" x 5"
2, 10, 13, 15	Dark pink	5" x 5"
3, 5, 7, 11, 14, 16	Medium pink	7" x 7"
4, 6, 8, 9, 17	Light pink	8" x 8"
19	Yellow	6" x 6"
Eyes	White	1" x 1"
	Black	1" x 1"

Doll

Shown at 100%

Follow General Directions to assemble doll.

Place the hair below "x" under face. Above "x," position hair on top of face.

Cut, place, and glue eye pieces— white, then black. Narrowly satin stitch white and black pieces.

Free-motion stitch around eyes and mouth two times, following the same stitching lines. Form nose when stitching left eye. Free-motion stitch eyebrows.

Drum

Appliqué Piece	Color	Piece Size
1, 2, 5, 6, 10	Gold	7" x 7"
3	Red	4" x 5"
4	Light tan	3" x 5"
7, 8, 9	Light gold	3" x 6"
Cording	Gold	16"

Follow General Directions to assemble drum except pieces 1 and 2. Cut these exact pattern size and set aside.

Satin stitch pieces 7, 8, and 9 onto piece 6, covering the entire width of these straps.

Glue gold cording into position and allow to dry; zigzag down.

After toys are arranged onto toy bag liner (see page 85 for layout), place, glue, and stitch drumsticks (pieces 1 and 2) before adding drum.

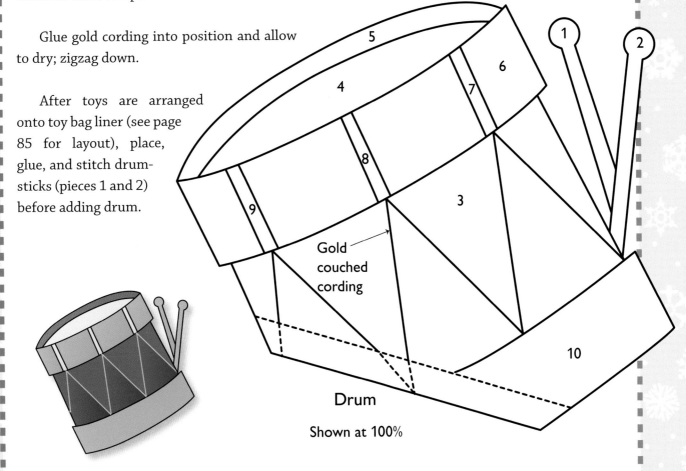

Gold couched cording

Drum

Shown at 100%

Football

Appliqué Piece	Color	Piece Size
1, 2	Copper	6" x 6"
3	Medium orange	4" x 4"
4	White cording	16"

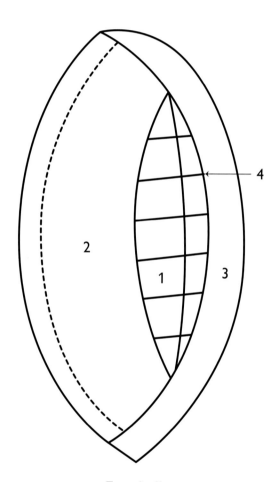

Follow General Directions to assemble football. Cut piece 1 adding ¼" seam lines all around. Mark cording lines and glue cording onto all short lines and long line; allow to dry. Satin stitch cording lines into place.

Prepare appliqué pieces 2 and 3.

Place and glue piece 1 to 2. Stitch this seam line by hand or machine. Add prepared piece 3.

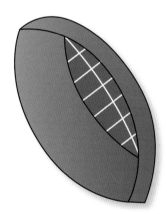

Football

Shown at 100%

Guitar

Appliqué Piece	Color	Piece Size
1	Beige	6" x 6"
2, 3, 4, 5	Black	6" x 6"
Cording	White	45"

Follow General Directions to assemble guitar.

Use black thread stitching to create top curved design, circles around the center, and three small circles under guitar strings. Crystals add interest.

Mark string lines using fabric marking pen. Place and glue strings; let dry. Satin stitch strings, just covering cording.

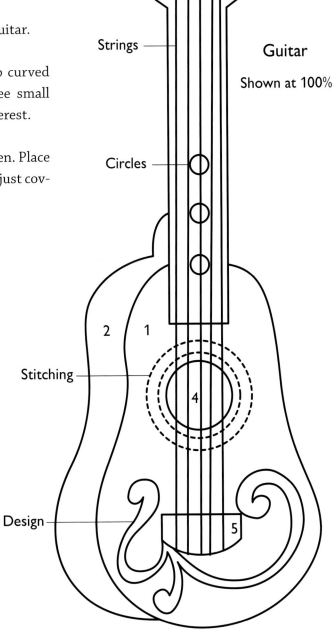

Strings

Guitar

Shown at 100%

Circles

Stitching

Design

Horn

Appliqué Piece	Color	Piece Size
1, 2, 4	Dark yellow	4" x 4"
3	Gold	6" x 6"
5	Light yellow	3" x 4"

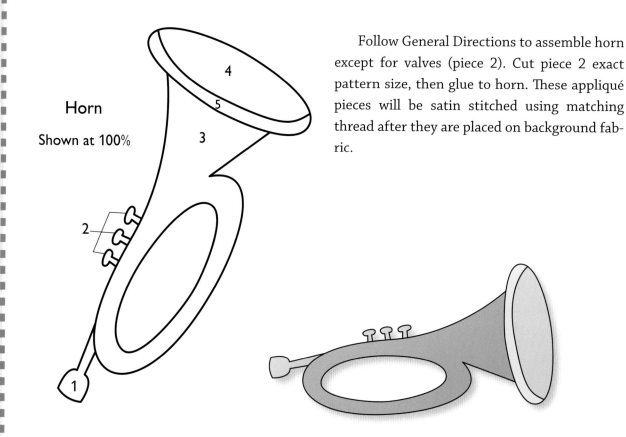

Horn

Shown at 100%

Follow General Directions to assemble horn except for valves (piece 2). Cut piece 2 exact pattern size, then glue to horn. These appliqué pieces will be satin stitched using matching thread after they are placed on background fabric.

Nutcracker

Appliqué Piece	Color	Piece Size
1, 2, 18, 20	Black	5" x 6"
3, 7, 11	Red	5" x 6'
4, 5, 8, 9, 12, 13, 14, 15, 16, 19	Gold	6" x 6"
6, 10, 17	Flesh	4" x 4'
Eyes	White	1" x 2"
	Blue	1" x 1"
Moustache	Black	1" x 2"

Follow General Directions to assemble nutcracker except cut decorative trim pieces 12, 13, and 14 exact shape of pattern.

Cut pieces 3 and 7 full length of sleeve adding ¼" seam allowances. Cut gold pieces 4, 5, 8, and 9 to fit freezer paper template. Place and glue. Turn under long outside edges of 3 and 7 using template. Follow General Directions to prepare all other remaining pieces except facial features and numbers 12, 13, and 14.

Cut round white eyes; glue blue pieces into place. Place and glue eyes to face. Glue mouth into place, noting small seam allowance to be added at top of lip. Cut moustache exact pattern size, then place and glue. Satin stitch narrowly around all features.

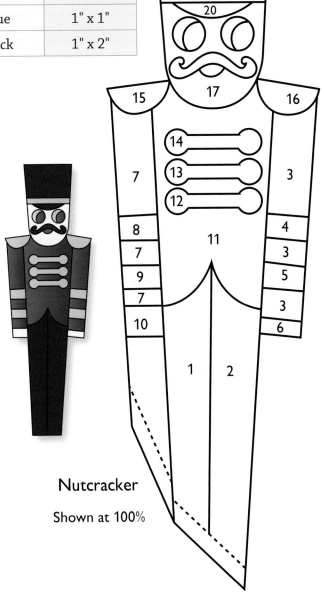

Nutcracker

Shown at 100%

Panda

APPLIQUÉ PIECE	COLOR	PIECE SIZE
1, 8	White	7" x 10"
2, 3, 6, 7, 9, 10, 14	Black	8" x 8"
4, 5, 11, 12	Brown	3" x 5"
13	Ivory	3" x 3"
15, 16, 19	Dark purple	3" x 4"
17, 20	Light purple	3" x 3"
18, 21	Medium purple	3" x 4"

Follow General Directions to assemble panda.

Place, glue, and hand stitch nose into place. Draw mouth lines under nose using fabric marking pen. Stitch mouth area two times, following same stitching line, beginning and ending at lower point of nose.

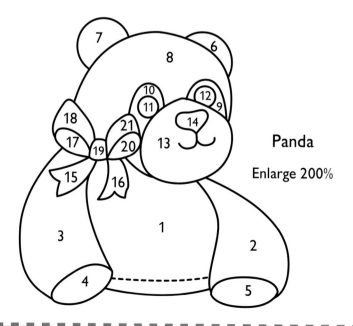

Panda

Enlarge 200%

Raggedy Ann Doll

APPLIQUÉ PIECE	COLOR	PIECE SIZE
1	Light green	3" x 4"
2, 4, 6, 10	Medium green	5" x 5"
3, 5	Medium dark green	4" x 5"
7, 11, 13, 15	Dark red	6" x 6"
8, 12, 14, 16	Bright yellow	4" x 4"
9	Bright blue	2" x 3"
17, 20, 24, 29	Dark red	6" x 6"
18, 22, 25, 27	Medium red	6" x 6"
19, 21, 23, 26, 28	Light red	7" x 7"
30	Pale yellow	4" x 4"
Eyes	Red	2" x 2"
Mouth	Black	1" x 1"

Follow General Directions to assemble Raggedy Ann doll except facial features.

Cut facial features exact pattern size. Place, glue, and narrowly satin stitch all features using black thread. Add satin-stitched bow tie.

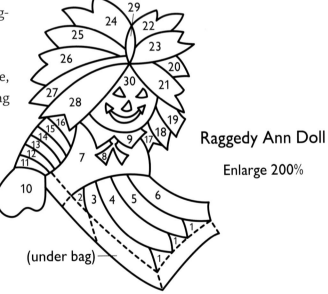

(under bag)

Raggedy Ann Doll

Enlarge 200%

Sailboat

Appliqué Piece	Color	Piece Size
1, 3	Light yellow	4" x 4"
2, 7, 12	Red	5" x 5"
4, 5	Gray or silver	2" x 7"
6, 8, 10, 13	Bright yellow	6" x 6"
9, 11	Royal blue	6" x 6"
14	Dark tan	4" x 6"

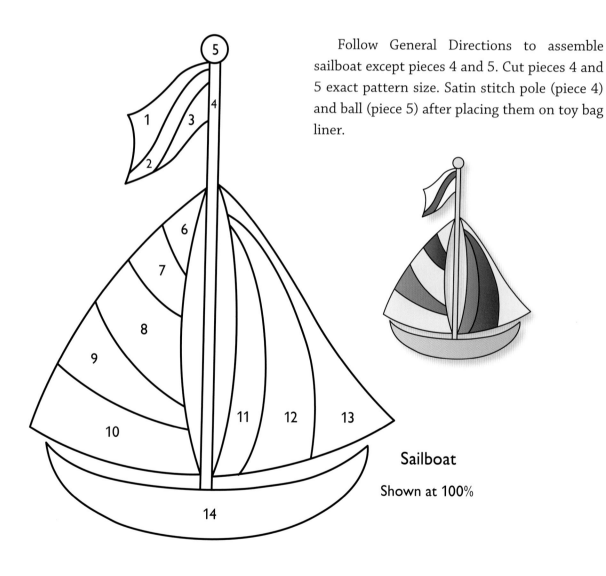

Follow General Directions to assemble sailboat except pieces 4 and 5. Cut pieces 4 and 5 exact pattern size. Satin stitch pole (piece 4) and ball (piece 5) after placing them on toy bag liner.

Sailboat

Shown at 100%

Skis

APPLIQUÉ PIECE	COLOR	PIECE SIZE
1	White	4" x 8"
2	Ivory	3" x 5"
3	Red	2" x 2"

Follow General Directions to assemble skis. Cut stars (piece 3) exact pattern size. Place, glue, and stitch.

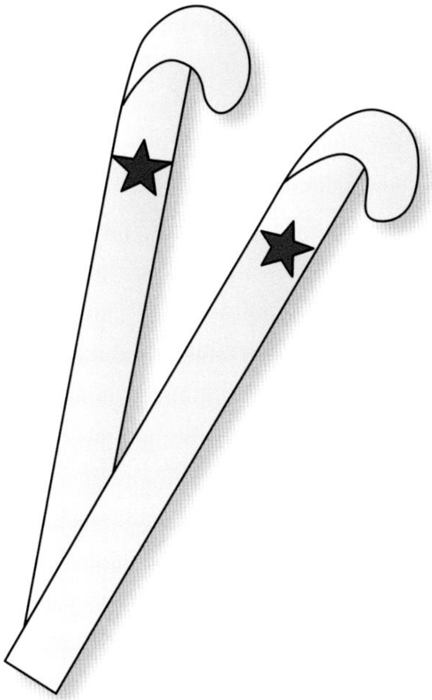

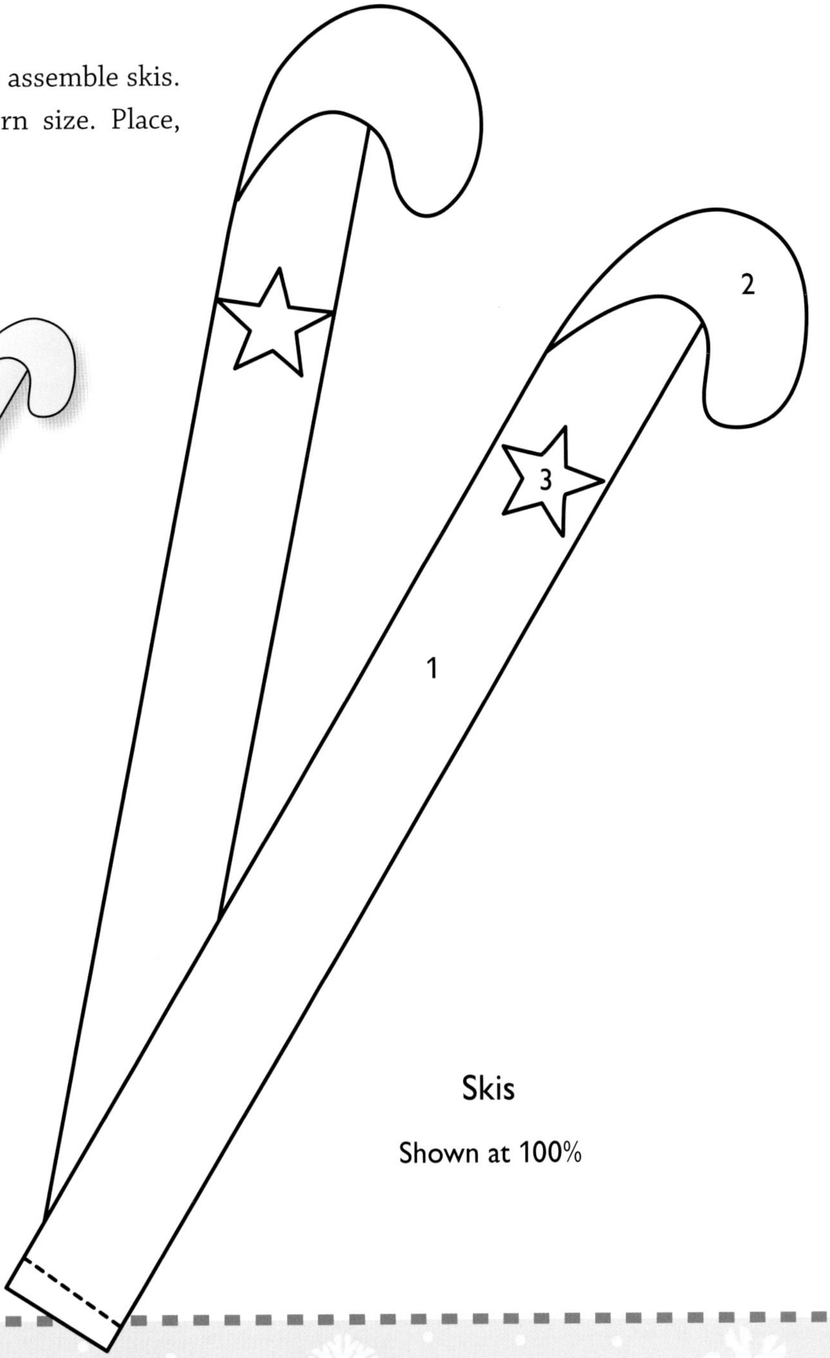

Skis

Shown at 100%

Spinning Top

Appliqué Piece	Color	Piece Size
1, 5	Medium green	3" x 3"
2	Medium blue	3" x 4"
3	Red	3" x 4"
4	Bright yellow	3" x 3"
6	Rust	1" x 1"
7	Orange	1" x 1"

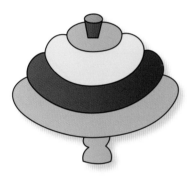

Follow General Directions to assemble spinning top. A portion of the spinning top is placed under panda; outer right edge is placed on top of toy bag lip.

Spinning Top

Shown at 100%

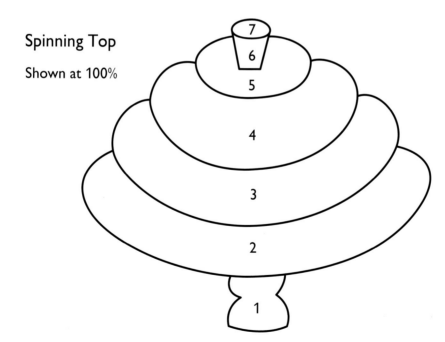

Teddy Bear

Appliqué Piece	Color	Piece Size
1, 4, 8	Medium brown	4" x 4"
2, 6	Medium tan	5" x 6"
3, 5	Dark brown	2" x 3"
7	Light tan	3" x 3"
11	White	2" x 2"
9, 10, 12	Black	1" x 2"

Follow General Directions to assemble teddy bear except numbers 9, 10, and 12.

Cut eyes and nose exact pattern size, then place and glue into position. Narrowly satin stitch using black thread. Free-motion stitch to form smile, beginning at the center of nose. Stitch lines two times.

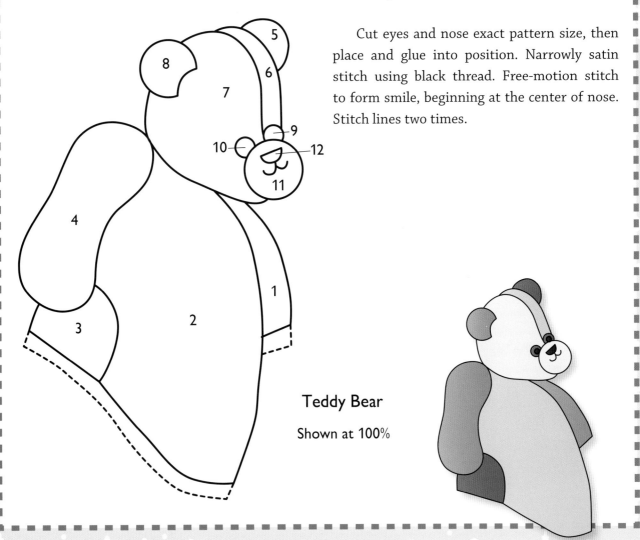

Teddy Bear

Shown at 100%

Teddy Bear with Vest

APPLIQUÉ PIECE	COLOR	PIECE SIZE
1, 4, 6, 11, 16, 18	Dark purple	6" x 6"
2, 3, 5, 7, 13, 17	Medium purple	6" x 6"
8, 9	Light yellow	4" x 4"
10	Bright yellow	1" x 2"
12, 14, 15	Light purple	3" x 3"
Eyes, nose	Black	1" x 2"

Follow General Directions to assemble teddy bear with vest except nose, mouth, and eyes. Cut eyes and nose exact pattern size. Place and glue them on prepared pieces 13 and 15. Satin stitch narrowly. Eye seam allowance is placed under piece 15.

To create mouth, use black thread; begin stitching at lower point of nose. Double-stitch mouth using free motion.

Teddy Bear with Vest

Shown at 100%

Tennis Racquet

Appliqué Piece	Color	Piece Size
1	Same as quilt background	3" x 4"
3, 4	Red	5" x 6"
2	White cording	38"

Follow General Directions to assemble pieces 1, 3 and 4. Mark cording lines (2); then glue in place vertically, then horizontally. Let dry. Zigzag all lines in both directions.

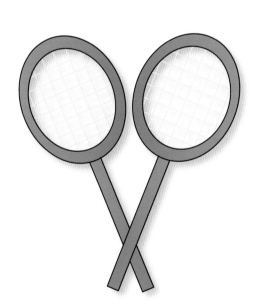

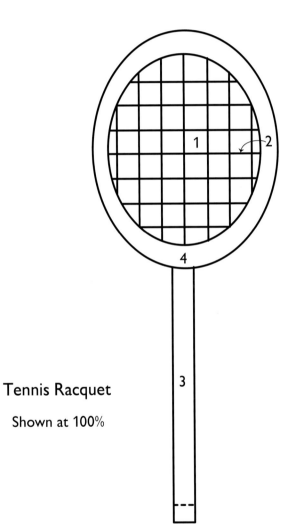

Tennis Racquet

Shown at 100%

Train

APPLIQUÉ PIECE	COLOR	PIECE SIZE
Train		
1, 5, 6, 8, 10, 12, 15, 17, 20, 22, 26, 27	Black	14" x 14"
2, 9, 11, 13, 19, 25	Medium gray	10" x 10"
3, 21, 23, 24	Light gray	14" x 14"
4, 7, 14, 16, 18	Red	10" x 10"
Wheels		
C, F, I	Black	6" x 6"
A, D, G, J, K	Medium gray	6" x 6"
B, E, H	Light gray	5" x 5"

Follow General Directions to assemble train. Assemble wheels separately. Place and glue connecting bars (pieces J and K). After toys are stitched onto inner bag, add wheels.

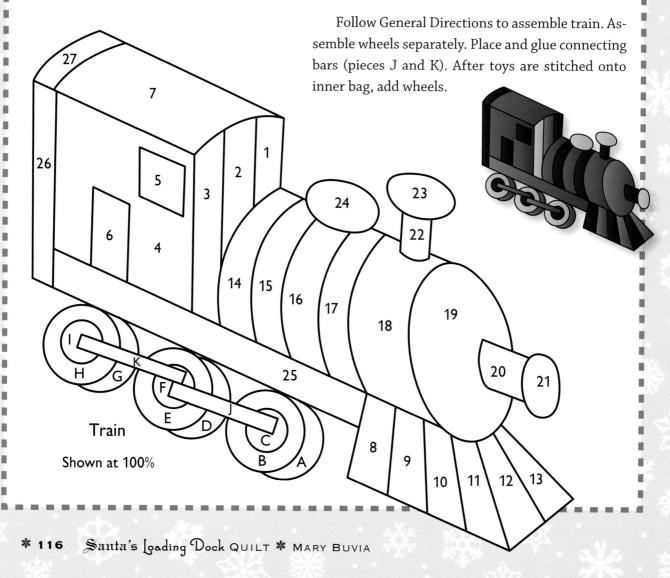

Train

Shown at 100%

Two Packages

APPLIQUÉ PIECE	COLOR	PIECE SIZE
Pink and green package		
1	Dark purple	3" x 6"
2	Light purple	4" x 5"
3, 5, 6, 7	Medium green	7" x 12"
4	Medium purple	4" x 6"
8, 10, 11	Dark green	3" x 4"
9, 12	Light green	4" x 5"
White and red package		
1, 4	Medium blue	8" x 8"
2	Light blue	6" x 6"
3, 5, 6, 14	Red	6" x 6"
7	Light red	4" x 4"
8, 10, 12	Medium green	6" x 6"
9, 11, 13	Light green	6" x 6"

Follow General Directions to assemble purple and green package. Decorate ribbons 3 and 5 with metallic threads, holly appliqués, or stripes.

Follow General Directions to assemble red and white package except holly and berry (pieces 8, 9, 10, 11, 12, 13, 14).

Form holly by using two colors. Cut exact outside shape; add ¼" seam allowance to center line. Turn under light green seam allowance. Place, glue, and stitch onto dark half of holly.

Package edge will be placed under the toy bag lip; holly will be placed on top of bag lip.

Two Packages

Purple and Green Package

Shown at 100%

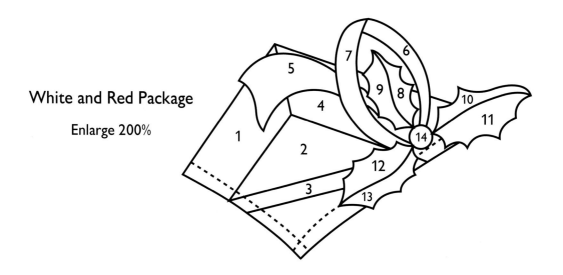

White and Red Package

Enlarge 200%

TOY SHOP

Order of Assembly

Follow General Directions to assemble appliqués unless otherwise directed.

Add the elf with gift on steps (see page 57) after adding the teddy bear.

See Color and
Yardage chart
on page 22.

Toy Shop Area

Enlarge 500%
Actual Size 51"

Blue/Lavender
Triangles and Board

Brick Walls

Appliqué Piece	Color	Piece Size
B	Light orange	16" x 16"
	Medium orange	16" x 16"
	Dark orange	16" x 16"
	Red	16" x 16"
C	Gray or silver	13" x 44"

Follow General Directions to create each wall either by piecing the sections or by cutting the gray background as 1 piece, using freezer paper technique.

Number and indicate color and grain line on each brick. Arrange the 4 brick colors for a pleasing effect. Place, glue, and stitch each brick into place. Trim excess gray background fabric.

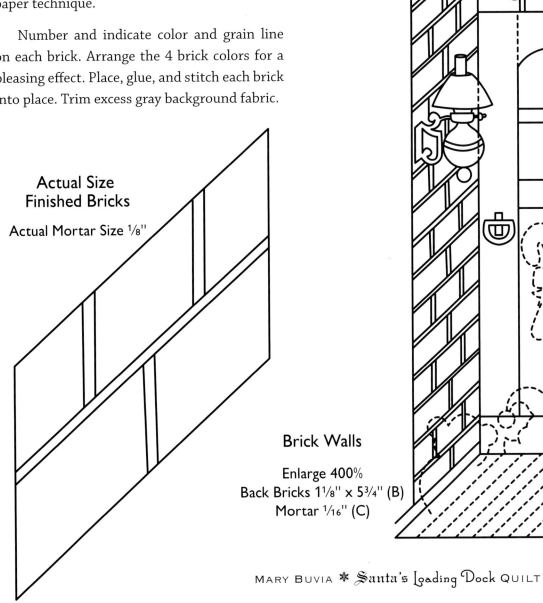

**Actual Size
Finished Bricks**

Actual Mortar Size ⅛"

Brick Walls

Enlarge 400%
Back Bricks 1⅛" x 5¾" (B)
Mortar 1⁄16" (C)

Door and Latch

APPLIQUÉ PIECE	COLOR	PIECE SIZE
Door		
1	Bright yellow	5" x 7"
2	Medium tan	5" x 8"
3	Dark tan	6" x 18"
4	Medium pink	5" x 10"
5	Gold	3" x 7"
Latch		
1	Red	1" x 1"
2	Black	2" x 2"

Door and Latch

Enlarge 400%
Actual Size 5⅝" x 18"

Follow General Directions to assemble door and latch.

Sew pieces 1 and 2; add pieces 3 (door top and bottom) and 4. Press seams. Add pieces 3 (door sides) and 5.

Create the door latch either by freezer paper or raw edge construction techniques. Place, glue, and stitch onto background.

Add latch to door. When completed, piece door top to brick wall with shop sign, then piece angled brick wall to door/brick section.

Candy Canes

APPLIQUÉ PIECE	COLOR	PIECE SIZE
Candy Canes		
1	White	4" x 12"
2	Red	4" x 12"
Bow		
3	Dark green	2" x 3"
4	Medium green	5" x 5"
5	Light green	2" x 2"

Follow General Directions to assemble candy canes appliqué.

Add seam allowances for red stripes (piece 2) only to outside (short) edges. Satin stitch both long edges of red fabric; do not stitch outside edges (short sides).

When complete, re-iron template onto reverse side of white/red candy canes, one at a time, carefully centering template over fabric. White excess fabric (behind red fabric) may be cut away after satin stitching is completed.

Add stitched bow to candy canes.

Place, glue, and stitch completed appliqué on background.

Stitch green lines on candy canes while quilting.

Candy Canes

Shown at 100%

Wall Lamp

APPLIQUÉ PIECE	COLOR	PIECE SIZE
2, 5	White	4" x 8"
3, 4	Red	3" x 3"
6, 7	Black	3" x 4"
1, 8	Light yellow	3" x 4"

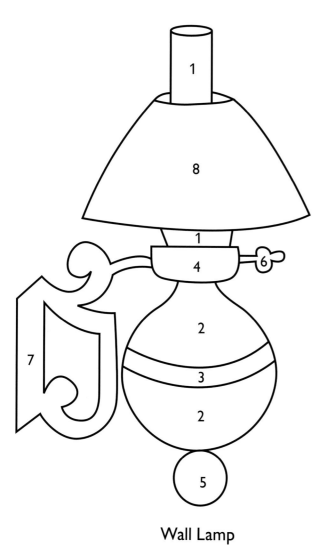

Follow General Directions to assemble lamp except pieces 6 and 7; cut them exact size.

Place, glue, and satin stitch pieces 6 and 7 onto background. Add remainder of appliqué. Trim away excess fabric to within ⅛" of seam lines.

Wall Lamp

Shown at 100%

"Shop"

Appliqué Piece	Color	Piece Size
1	White	3" x 10"
2, 3	Bright green	2" x 10"
4, 5	Medium dark green	6" x 10"
6	Red	2" x 9"

Follow General Directions to assemble pieces 1, 2, and 3. Turn under all edges of center white/ green piece. Set aside.

Cut letters exact pattern size. Satin stitch into place on piece 1.

Cut pieces 4 and 5 exact pattern size. Place and glue onto quilt top. Place and glue center section into place. Satin stitch pieces 4 and 5.

Remove excess fabric under center section only.

"Shop"

Enlarge 200%
Actual Size 4⅝" x 7⅞"

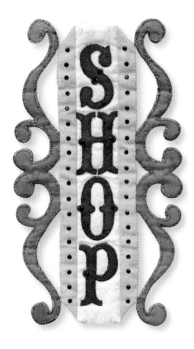

Wall Behind Sled and Stocking

Appliqué Piece	Color	Piece Size
1	Medium-dark purple	2" x 25"
2	Medium purple	2" x 26"
3	Medium-light purple	2" x 25"
4	Light purple	2" x 24"
5, 6	Dark purple	3" x 35"
7	Medium pink	5" x 13"

Cut and piece numbers 1, 2, 3, and 4. Press seams to dark sides. Add pieces 6 and 7. Add piece 5 and press seams. Piece left section of brick wall to completed wall behind sled. Add narrow angled board below stocking, leaving it unstitched where narrow left border A will be added.

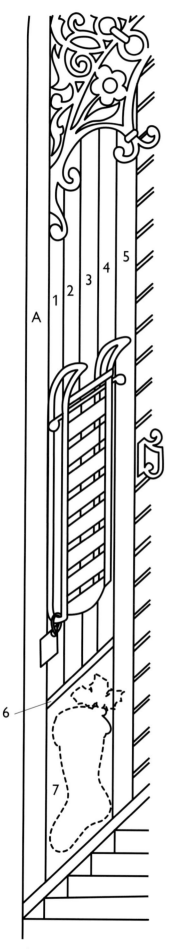

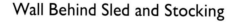

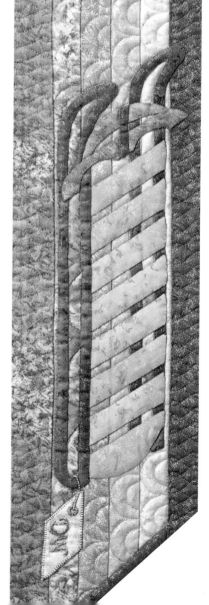

Wall Behind Sled and Stocking

Enlarge 400%
Actual Sizes
1 – ¾" x 23½"
2 – ¾" x 23¾"
3 – ¾" x 23½"
4 – ¾" x 22¾"
5 – ⅞" x 32"
7 – 3" x 8¾"

Sled

Appliqué Piece	Color	Piece Size
1	Dark green	3" x 3"
2, 3	Dark orange	6" x 12"
4	Light orange	3" x 3"
5, 6, 7, 8, 9, 10, 11, 12	Medium green	7" x 12"
13	White	2" x 2"
Cording	Green	1½"

Follow General Directions to assemble sled except pieces 1, 2, and 3. Cut these exact pattern size.

Place, glue, and stitch sled onto background.

Position gift tag and glue into place, leaving upper corner open. Place cording into position and stitch. Glue corner of name tag and stitch. Create circle eyelet when quilting.

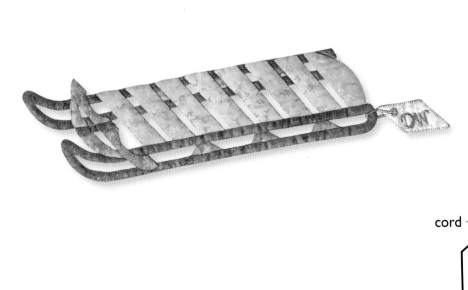

cord

Sled

Enlarge 200%

Stocking and Letters

Appliqué Piece	Color	Piece Size
1, 11	White	5" x 8"
2, 3, 5, 7, 9, 12, 13, 14	Red	8" x 8"
4, 6, 8, 10	Medium green	4" x 5"
15, 16, 17	Light green	4" x 5"
Stars	Light blue	5" x 5"
Letters	Gold	4" x 4"
Critter in Stocking		
Head, feet	Dark tan	1½" x 1½"
Eye band	Light tan	1" x 1¼"
Eyes, nose	Black	1" x 1"

Follow General Directions to assemble stocking except cut holly and berry pieces 12, 13, 14, 15, 16, and 17 exact size. Place and glue these sections onto background fabric after entire stocking appliqué is completed. Satin stitch holly pieces into place. Stitch stocking to background. Create division lines on holly during quilting.

Cut stars exact pattern size. Place, glue, and stitch onto stocking. Satin stitch into place.

Cut, place, and glue letters onto stars. Narrowly satin stitch. Another option is to satin stitch entire gold letter with decorative thread. Stitch slowly while adjusting the width to completely cover the fabric.

Cut all critter pieces exact pattern size except add ⅛" seam allowance to upper edges of feet. Glue onto completed stocking top; satin stitch all areas. Eyes and nose can be created with Pigma® pen, free-motion or hand embroidery, or appliqué.

On reverse side, remove all excess background fabric to within ¼" of seam lines.

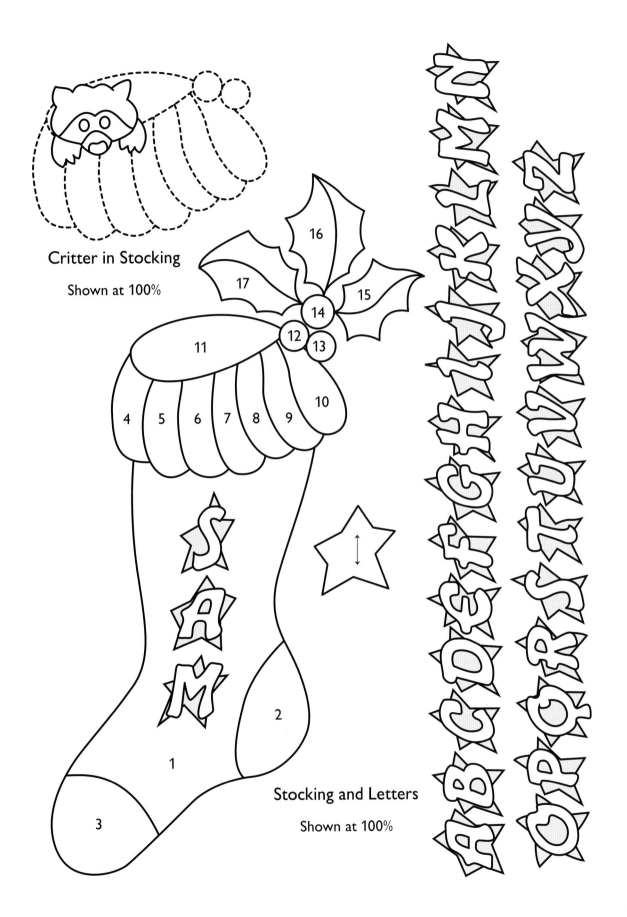

Critter in Stocking

Shown at 100%

Stocking and Letters

Shown at 100%

Landing and Steps

APPLIQUÉ PIECE	COLOR	PIECE SIZE
D	Light lavender	5" x 12"
1	Light lavender	2" x 15"
2	Medium-light lavender	2" x 15"
3	Medium lavender	2" x 14"
4	Medium-dark lavender	2" x 12"
5	Dark lavender	2" x 11"

Stitch triangle piece to each step; piece all 5 steps and press seams. Add D (landing). Dotted lines on landing indicate quilting design; other dotted lines indicate appliqué placement.

Landing and Steps

Enlarge 200%
Actual finished sizes:
- 1 – 1" x 13⅝"
- 2 – 1" x 12½"
- 3 – 1" x 11⅜"
- 4 – 1" x 10¼"
- 5 – 1" x 9⅛"

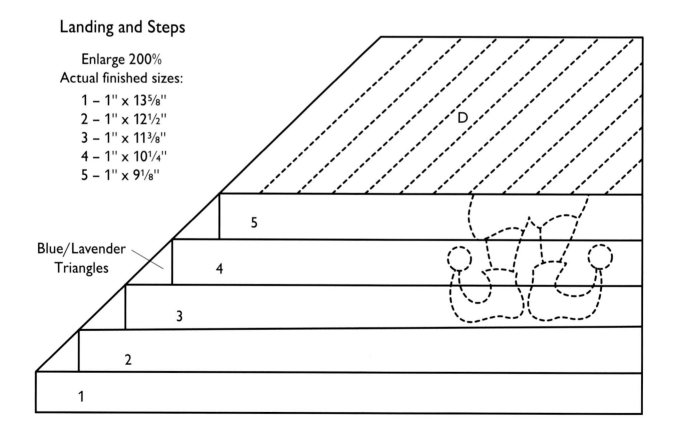

Background and Ironwork

Appliqué Piece	Color	Piece Size
1	Medium blue	16" x 24"
2	Gold	15" x 27"

Cut all ironwork sections to exact pattern size. Add ½" seam allowances to the right side; this is the edge of the quilt top. Also add ½" seam allowances to those areas that will be stitched into the left border seam lines; they will be trimmed to ¼" after stitching is complete.

Satin stitch pieces into place.

Blue background section will be cut as 1 piece, adding ½" allowance to the right, top, and left sides. The bottom edge should not extend beyond the gold ironwork. Satin stitch the completed ironwork to the brick and board walls.

Background and Ironwork

Enlarge 400%

Shop Sign Bell

APPLIQUÉ PIECE	COLOR	PIECE SIZE
1	Soft gold	2" x 4"
2	Medium green	2" x 3"
3	White	5" x 5"
4, 5	Medium or light green	5" x 5"
6	Gold	3" x 4"
7, 9	Dark green	4" x 4"
8, 10	Light green	4" x 4"
11	Red	1" x 1"

Follow General Directions to assemble bell except cut upper bell background (piece 3) as one piece, adding ¼" seam allowances. Do not turn under edges at this point until all ornamentation is stitched or appliquéd.

Cut pieces 4 and 5 with seam allowances on two narrow outer edges only; glue into position.

Use a wide zigzag satin stitch to cover the entire width of the fabric. Stitch to outer edge of fabric.

Follow the same process for piece 6.

Piece two sections of holly leaves down center. Raw-edge appliqué is used to stitch edges to background fabric. Center berry (piece 11) may be raw-edge stitched or seam allowance turned under with template.

Create circles (piece A) with appliqué or quilt them in.

After all designs are placed on bell, reapply template on reverse side to turn under outer seam allowances.

Place, glue, and stitch completed appliqué to background.

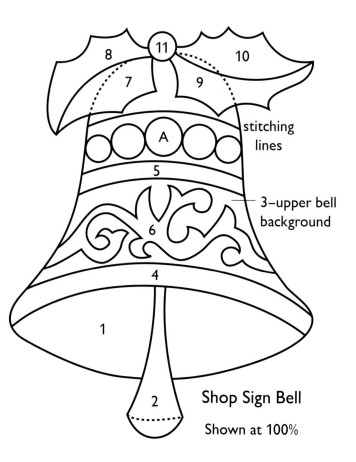

stitching lines

3–upper bell background

Shop Sign Bell

Shown at 100%

Left Narrow Purple Frame and Stone Wall

Appliqué Piece	Color	Piece Size
Background		
	Silver	18" x 60"
Left Border		
	Blue/lavender	15" x 60"
Stones (20 each)		
	Light beige	20" x 20"
	Light tan	20" x 20"
	Medium tan	20" x 20"
	Dark tan	20" x 20"
	Medium gray	20" x 20"

Follow General Directions to create stones. Arrange stone colors for a pleasing natural appearance. Number each stone and indicate color on both pattern and freezer paper template. Turn under all outside edges.

Cut background (silver) with seam allowances on inside edge only. Outside curved edge will be satin stitched onto left border (blue/lavender).

Place, glue, and stitch stones. Trim excess fabric from behind stones to within ¼" of seam lines.

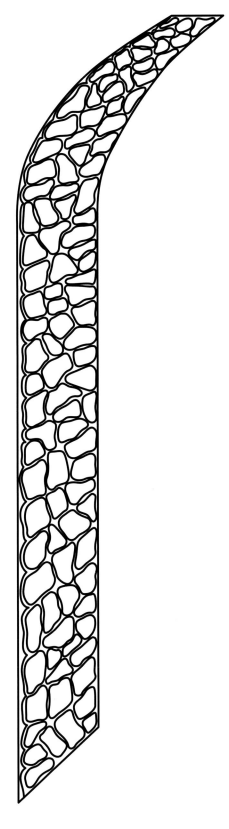

Left Narrow Purple Frame and Stone Wall

Enlarge 665%

Outside Border

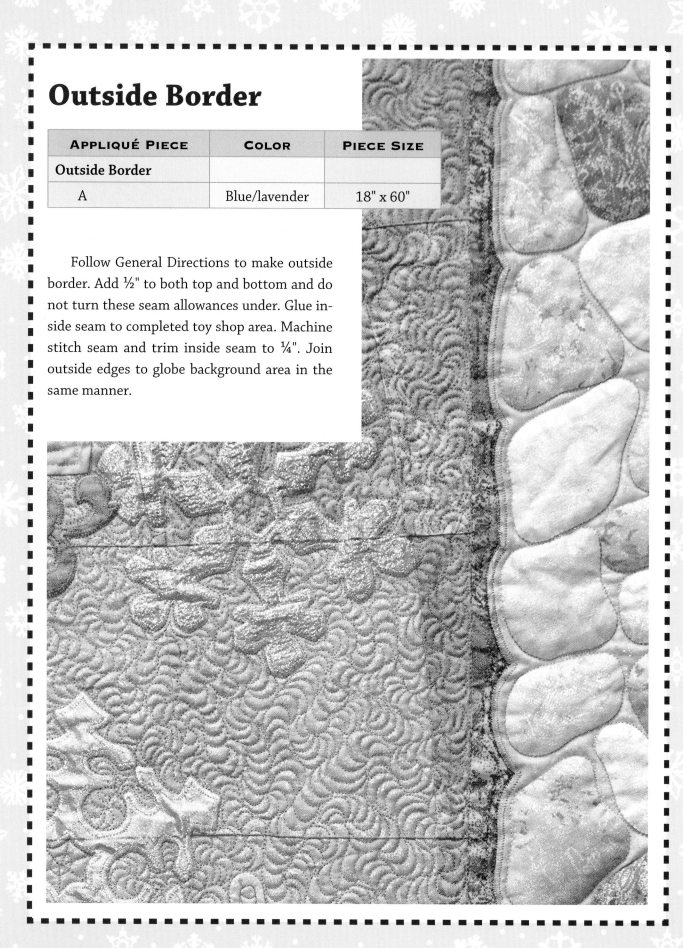

APPLIQUÉ PIECE	COLOR	PIECE SIZE
Outside Border		
A	Blue/lavender	18" x 60"

Follow General Directions to make outside border. Add ½" to both top and bottom and do not turn these seam allowances under. Glue inside seam to completed toy shop area. Machine stitch seam and trim inside seam to ¼". Join outside edges to globe background area in the same manner.

Teddy Bear on Steps

APPLIQUÉ PIECE	COLOR	PIECE SIZE
Teddy		
1, 7	Medium tan	3" x 6"
2, 3, 5	Light tan	5" x 6"
4, 6, 9, 10, 12	Black	4" x 4"
8	Dark tan	4" x 4"
11, 13, 14	White	3" x 3"
Package		
A	Medium pink	4" x 4"
B	Dark pink	4" x 4"

Follow General Directions to assemble teddy. Trim excess fabric to within ⅛" of seam lines. Cut nose and eyes exact pattern size except add small allowance to be placed under piece 11. Satin stitch nose and eyes. Stitch mouth with free-motion technique.

Use freezer paper or raw-edge technique to create package and ribbon. Place, glue, and stitch to teddy.

Place, glue, and stitch completed appliqué to background.

Teddy Bear on Steps

Enlarge 200%

WINDOW

Order of Assembly

Please read through this entire section to better understand
the order of assembly.

Window Background

APPLIQUÉ PIECE	COLOR	PIECE SIZE
1	Dark blue	30" x 42"
2	White	8" x 25"
3	Yellowish white	9" x 15"
4	Bluish white	8" x 25"
5	White	9" x 20"
6 thru 38, N, O, E, L	Gold	2 yards
Window trim	Dark gold	18" x 18"

Follow General Directions to assemble window except as noted below.

Cut dark blue background (piece 1) adding ½" seam allowance around entire perimeter. Use a light box to see pattern through dark fabric.

For snow pieces 2, 3, and 4, cut and press down seam allowances to be stitched. Do not add dark blue top until seam lines are stitched by hand or machine. Glue top of snow line to dark blue background. Stitch into place.

Cut icicles exact pattern size. If delicate fabric is used, add Steam-a-Seam Lite to reverse side following manufacturer's directions. If cotton fabric is used, place and glue perimeter of icicles onto background fabric. Satin stitch icicles into place. No need to remove any background fabric behind icicles. Straight stitch ¼" top curve to join two icicles with blue background.

A number of other appliqués must be completed to finish the window:

Place and glue completed snowman into place (see page 141). Lower edge of snowman will be included in the snow seam. Do not trim excess background fabric until piece 1 is added to snow (piece 4).

Position background fabric onto master pattern, matching all lines. Place and glue completed star (see page 147), completed tree (see page 142), and Rudy (see page 143–146). Satin stitch edges of star. Trim excess fabric from back side close to stitching.

Add candle (see page 149) after windowpanes (see pages 137–138) are in place but before bottom window ledge (see page 138) is added. Add holly (see page 150) to candle after window is completed.

Windowpanes

Add gold windowpane lines in numerical order (see pattern on page 139). Carefully cut freezer paper templates for windowpane

Window Background

divisions, as these forms will create the exact shape of finished panes. Templates may be re-used up to 8 times.

Place N – O – E – L cut letters in position. Note that tops and bottoms of N, E, and L will have ¼" seam allowances to be placed under horizontal panes. Cut the O with no seam allowances; place on top of horizontal windowpanes. Stitch O only after windowpanes 9 and 10 are added.

Place stabilizer behind letters and satin stitch using decorative threads for sparkle effect. Excess background fabric may be cut away behind letters to within ¼" of seam line.

With entire background pinned into place on master pattern, place and glue window panes in the following order:

1. Numbers 6 and 7 may be cut as individual panes, or cut the entire strip, if desired.
2. Add 8, 9, and 10.
3. Add 11 and 12.
4. Add 13.
5. Add 14 and 5 (entire length).
6. Add 16, 17, 18, 19, and 20.
7. Add 21, 22, 23, 24, 25, 26, 27, 28, 29, and 30 (outside top curve).
8. Add 31 (inside top curve). Piece 31 may be pieced to numbers 32 and 33 at the indicated dotted lines. Place and glue the entire unit to background.
9. Add 34 (outside top curve).
10. Add 35 (inside oval around star).

11. Prepare freezer paper template for bottom pieces 36, 37, and 38, leaving top seam allowances open on 36 and 37. Place and glue 36 to 37; glue 37 to 38 following master pattern. Machine stitch the two seams.

Add candle appliqué at this time. Glue into position except lower holly. Place and glue piece 38 down to holly; lift bottom of leaf and continue to glue on top of candle holder and out to edge of piece 32. Stitch seam line (38).

Glue lower holly to piece 38. With stabilizer behind all holly, satin stitch. Remove stabilizer. Remainder of candle may be hand stitched. On reverse side, clip excess fabric to within ¼" of seam lines.

All gold window separations may be hand or machine stitched into place. On reverse side, trim all seam lines to within ¼" of stitching. Completed window may be placed and glued on quilt top and hand stitched into position. Cut away excess quilt top fabric on reverse side to within ¼" of seam line.

Window Trim

Secure Steam-a-Seam onto back side of fabric following manufacturer's directions. Pin actual paper patterns onto fabric using very short straight pins. Cut the exact shape of the trim. Place and iron into position on quilt top. Place tear-away stabilizer behind fabric. Satin stitch. Remove stabilizer. No trimming on reverse side is necessary.

Window

Enlarge 400%

Window Trim

Enlarge 200%

Left   Right

Window Trim
(Lower Section)

Enlarge 200%

Snowman

APPLIQUÉ PIECE	COLOR	PIECE SIZE
1, 2, 4, 5, 10, 15, 17, 19	White	8" x 8"
3, 6, 7, 8, 14, 16, 18	Black	6" x 6"
11, 12	Red	1" x 1"
13	Green	1" x 1"
9	Orange	1" x 1"

Follow General Directions to assemble snowman except for pieces 3, 6, 7, 8, and 9. Cut these exact pattern size.

Place, glue, and stitch appliqué.

Place and glue pieces 3, 6, 7, and 8. Narrowly satin stitch these pieces.

Stitch carrot nose after snowman is placed and glued on background fabric. Stitch slowly in order to adjust width of satin stitch as necessary.

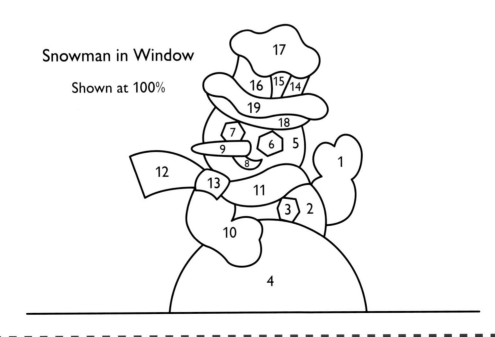

Snowman in Window

Shown at 100%

Tree in Window

Appliqué Piece	Color	Piece Size
2, 5, 9, 12, 22, 25, 27, 28, 34, 37	Light green	8" x 12"
1, 3, 11, 16, 39	Light blue	6" x 6"
4, 6, 7, 14, 17, 19, 21, 23, 26, 29, 30, 35, 41	Ivory	8" x 12"
8, 10, 13, 15, 18, 20, 24, 31, 32, 33, 36, 38, 40, 42	White	9" x 12"

Follow General Directions to assemble tree.

Place, glue, and stitch entire tree. Place and glue tree onto background fabric; stitch perimeter. Trim out excess background fabric to within ¼" of seam line.

Create definition between sections by quilting in the ditch. Some areas will require backtracking to minimize start/stop locations.

Tree in Window

Enlarge 200%

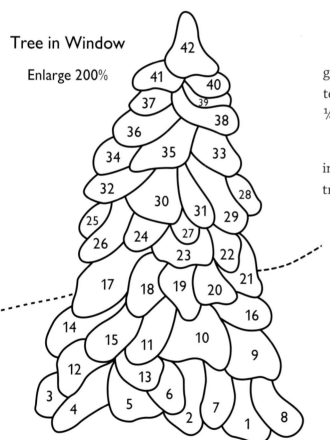

Rudy and Name Tag

APPLIQUÉ PIECE	COLOR	PIECE SIZE
Left Antler and Ribbon		
1, 3, 5, 7, 9, 11, 12	Medium brown	7" x 7"
2, 4, 6, 8	Light brown	7" x 7"
10	Red	2" x 5"
Right Antler and Ribbon		3" x 4"
1, 2, 4, 5, 6, 8, 9, 15	Medium brown	7" x 7"
3, 7, 10, 14, 16	Light brown	7" x 8"
11, 13	Light red	4" x 7"
10, 12	Dark red	2" x 3"
Rudy		
2, 3, 5, 7	Black	3" x 5"
1	Medium brown	5" x 6"
4, 11	Medium tan	2" x 4"
6	White	2" x 2"
8, 9	Light pink	2" x 2"
10	Red	1" x 2"
Name Tag		
A	Light green	2" x 3"
B	Light blue	2" x 3"
C	Red	2" x 3"

Follow General Directions to assemble Rudy except pieces 5, 6, 7, 11 (Rudy's face and top hair), face and body outline (piece 1), and name (Rudy). Place, glue, and stitch appliqué.

Cut pieces listed above exact pattern size. Position and glue into place. Satin stitch. Using black thread, free-motion straight stitch around eyes and mouth three times, following same stitching line. Extend the stitching to include the smile lines. Using the same method, stitch eyebrows.

Hand stitch prepared and glued areas of face and antlers.

Cut right and left ribbons exact pattern size. Place, glue, and satin stitch. Before stitching ribbons, glue bell hangers into place.

To form the name "Rudy," cut and satin stitch each letter or use embroidery.

For name tag background, cut piece B full size of combined A and B pieces adding no seam allowance. Cut piece A with no seam allowance; glue to piece B. Satin stitch the full width of fabric A. Stitch slowly and adjust the width around corners to cover all edges. Add name letters and stitch.

Place and glue completed appliqué, including ornaments and bells, on background. Satin stitch the ribbons, top hair (piece 11), and entire piece 1.

Dotted lines indicate window panes positioned over Rudy appliqué.

Rudy and Name Tag

Enlarge 200%

Left Antler and ribbon
1–10

Right Antler and ribbon
1–13

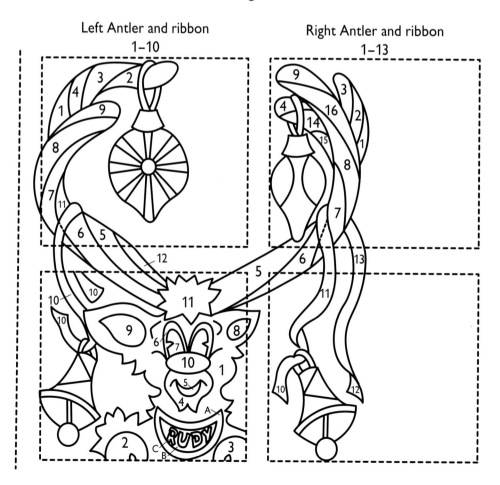

Rudy's Ornaments and Bells

APPLIQUÉ PIECE	COLOR	PIECE SIZE
Left Antler Ornament A*		
1	Color to contrast with red and green	4" x 4"
2, 3, 4, 5, 6, 7, 8, 9, 12	Red	5" x 5"
10	Green	1" x 1"
11	Red *(if fabric; 5" cording may be used)*	1" x 1"
Right Antler Ornament B*		
1	Purple	3" x 4"
2, 3, 5	Red	5" x 5"
4	Red *(if fabric; 4" cording may be used)*	2" x 2"
Left & Right Ribbon Bells C and D**		
1	Light gold	2" x 2"
2, 3	Medium gold	2" x 2"
4	Medium gold *(if fabric; 3" cording may be used)*	2" x 2"
5, 7	Light gold	2" x 3"
6	Light green	2" x 3"
8	Medium green	2" x 3"

*Optional: A decorative fabric may be fussy cut to create ornaments A and B, as in THE LOADING DOCK.

**Yardage is listed for bell C. Bell D pattern is simply reversed. Use same yardage figure in your choice of colors.

Rudy's Ornaments and Bells

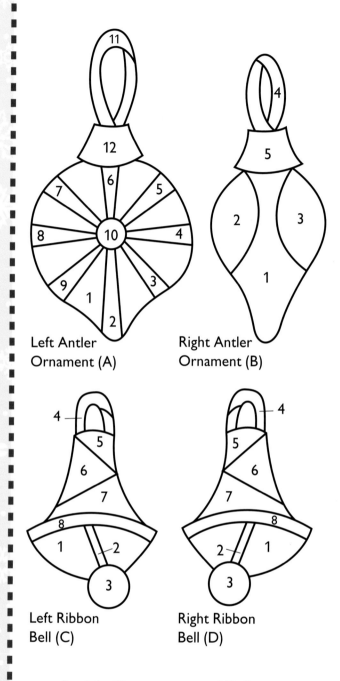

Left Antler
Ornament (A)

Right Antler
Ornament (B)

Left Ribbon
Bell (C)

Right Ribbon
Bell (D)

Rudy's Ornaments and Bells

Shown at 100%

Follow General Directions to assemble pieces 1 and 12. Do not turn edges under at this time.

Cut pieces 2 through 9 exact pattern size, adding ¼" seam allowances for two short ends only. Place and glue onto piece 1. Narrowly satin stitch narrowly all long sides.

Place, glue, and stitch piece 10. Trim excess fabric on back side of circle.

Carefully place freezer paper pattern (piece 1), iron into place, and turn under outside seam allowances. Place, glue, and stitch piece 12. Create piece 11 with fabric or cord.

Follow General Directions to assemble bells. For hanger, see directions for ornament A.

Star

Appliqué Piece	Color	Piece Size
1	White	8" x 8"
2, 3, 4, 5	Light yellow	6" x 12"
6, 7, 8, 9, 10	Light blue	5" x 5"

Review General Directions. Draw outside star shape and inside triangles 2, 3, 4, and 5 with marking pen. Do not cut outside star shape until triangles have been reverse appliquéd.

To reverse appliqué inside triangles, cut these 4 shapes carefully away from star. Cut 2 light yellow triangles, adding ¼" seam allowances on all sides for pieces 2, 3, 4, and 5. Cut 5 light blue triangles, adding ¼" seam allowances on all sides for pieces 6, 7, 8, 9, and 10.

Glue from top side of triangles to adhere yellow and blue fabric to star fabric. Press triangles with warm iron to dry quickly. Satin stitch. Remove stabilizer and trim all excess fabric close to seam line on reverse side.

Cut outside star shape exact size. Glue into place on background fabric. Satin stitch entire perimeter. Cut away excess background fabric to within ⅛" of stitching line.

Create dotted stitching lines (light rays) during quilting. For best ray definition, begin stitching at point of star to outer edge of line and then back to point of star. Shorter lines may be added for a glowing effect.

Star

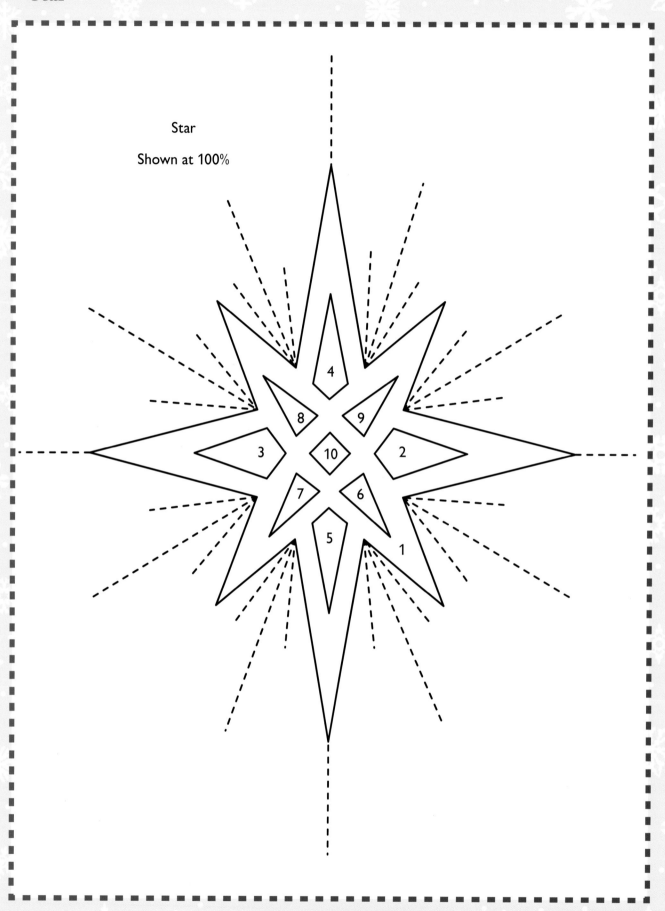

Star

Shown at 100%

Candle

APPLIQUÉ PIECE	COLOR	PIECE SIZE
1	Medium red	2" x 3"
2	Light red	2" x 4"
3	Dark red	2" x 4"
4	Medium peach	3" x 3"
5	Pale yellow	2" x 3"
6	Bright yellow	2" x 3"
7	Bright orange	2" x 2"
8	Pale yellow	6" x 6"
9	Bronze/copper	2" x 2"
10	Bright red	2" x 2"
11, 11a	Light green, dark green	2" x 3"
12, 12a	Light-medium green, dark-medium green	2" x 3"
13, 13a	Light-light green, dark-light green	2" x 3"
Holly leaves option	Center lines may be simply quilted if solid color leaves are selected. If divided colors are selected, see figures 1 – 3.	2" x 2"

Follow General Directions to assemble candle except for pieces 7, 11, 12, and 13. Cut holly leaves and flame center to exact size; satin stitch. Use orange metallic thread on piece 7 for a beautiful glow. Use Glitter by Superior Threads on holly leaves for a festive appearance.

Glue, place, and sew piece 8 onto background fabric; add completed candle.

Candle

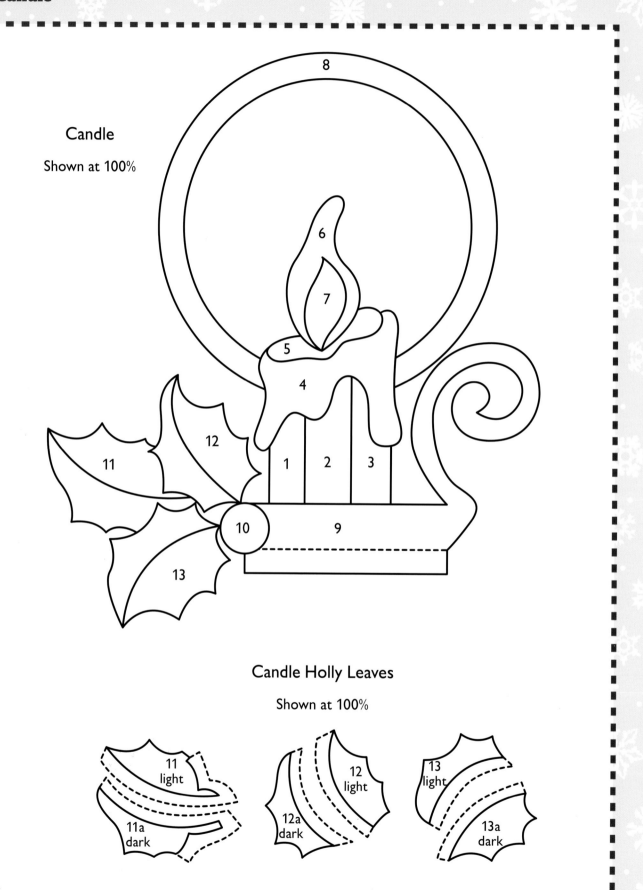

Candle

Shown at 100%

8

6

7

5

4

12

11

1   2   3

10   9

13

Candle Holly Leaves

Shown at 100%

11
light

11a
dark

12
light

12a
dark

13
light

13a
dark

Meet Mary Buvia

As I began my quiltmaking career in 1992 after years of sewing and owning businesses, I knew nothing about this art form and did not even realize classes were available. A friend told me about an organization called American Quilter's Society. I joined in an effort to learn all that I could through their published information. It changed my life as I began learning and quilting.

After making all the mistakes possible as a self-taught quilter, slowly I began getting it right after serious consideration of judges' comments when I entered shows.

For over a decade I have been teaching different techniques that work for me to both beginning and advanced quilters. My goals in classes are to help my students avoid all the mistakes that I have made. I am very proud to watch my students advance and achieve their personal goals. As I continue to reach my own goals, I feel it is our duty and pleasure to pass on the knowledge that we have gained to future generations of quilters.

I wish everyone success and personal satisfaction with each and every project. I can promise that each piece created will be better than the last.

I live in Greenwood, Indiana, with my six feline friends and eight friendly raccoons that visit us daily for a handout.

Please visit me at **www.marybuvia.com**.

more AQS Books

This is only a small selection of the books available from the American Quilter's Society. AQS books are known worldwide for timely topics, clear writing, beautiful color photos, and accurate illustrations and patterns. The following books are available from your local bookseller, quilt shop, or public library.

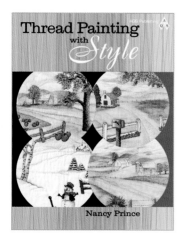

#8354

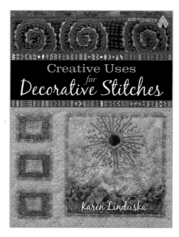

#8762

#8764

#8532

#8763

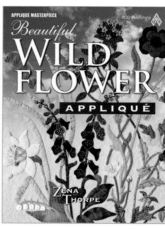

#8526

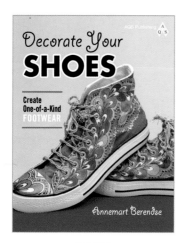

#8766

#8671

#8663

LOOK for these books nationally.
CALL or **VISIT** our website at

1-800-626-5420
www.AmericanQuilter.com